the
☐ bucket
☑ f＊ck it
☐ done it
list

To JK

Be S-M-R-T when using this list. Do not put yourself in peril or
harm's way or jeopardy or precarious positions. Use prudence and
circumspection and heedfulness and discretion when necessary.

10 9 8 7 6 5 4 3 2 1

Pop Press, an imprint of Ebury Publishing,
20 Vauxhall Bridge Road,
London SW1V 2SA

Pop Press is part of the Penguin Random House group of companies
whose addresses can be found at global.penguinrandomhouse.com

Penguin
Random House
UK

First published in the United States by Clarkson Potter Publishers, an imprint of the
Crown Publishing Group, a division of Penguin Random House LLC, New York.
First published in United Kingdom by Pop Press 2019

www.penguin.co.uk

A CIP catalogue record for this book is available from the British Library

ISBN 9781529104745

Printed and bound in Great Britain by Clays Ltd, Elcograf S.p.A.

Penguin Random House is committed to a sustainable future
for our business, our readers and our planet. This book is made
from Forest Stewardship Council® certified paper.

the
☐ **bucket**
☑ **f*ck it**
☐ **done it**
list

3669 things to do.
or not. whatever.

SARA KINNINMONT

**Illustrated by
Jamie Armstrong**

POP PRESS

1

SUPER FINE TURNIP WINE

80% OFF
UPPER LIP WAXING

Do you dream of seeing a honey badger in the wild? Cooking a three-bird roast? Visiting the town of Clit, Romania? Mastering Cockney rhyming slang? Wearing lederhosen? Drinking banana wine in the Canary Islands? Then this book is for you.

If you'd rather drink your own urine than do any of that, content instead to stay home and binge-watch Netflix, then this book is also for you.

Maybe you have a serious case of FOMO and are looking for new places to travel, foods to eat, art to see, or just want some legit social media fodder (spoiler: this book is for you, too).

Not your typical list book, *The Bucket/F*ck it List* lets you check off "bucket", "f*ck it", or "done it" for each of the 3,669 items, depending on whether you intend to do it, couldn't care less/would rather die than do it, or have already accomplished it.

Explore the list from front to back, back to front, or by plunging in at random. Whatever feels good to you. Don't be afraid to look up unfamiliar things. It will only enhance your experience. You'll see. Checking off shit just feels good.

☐ ☐ ☐ believe as many as six impossible things before breakfast

☐ ☐ ☐ use Cockney rhyming slang with ease

☐ ☐ ☐ see a honey badger in the wild

☐ ☐ ☐ practise parkour

☐ ☐ ☐ compete in the Mobile Phone Throwing World Championships in Finland

☐ ☐ ☐ collect black velvet paintings

☐ ☐ ☐ hike along the Ligurian Sea in Cinque Terre, Italy

☐ ☐ ☐ play in a cover band

☐ ☐ ☐ hiss at your nemesis

☐ ☐ ☑ identify as a Whovian

☐ ☐ ☐ drink fresh donkey milk on the street in Santiago, Chile

☐ ☐ ☐ throw a boomerang and catch it when it comes back to you

bucket
f*ck it
done it

☐ ☐ ☐ chew *saunf* instead of gum after a meal

☐ ☐ ☐ search for fairies at Pennard Castle in Swansea, Wales

☐ ☐ ☐ start off your Sunday with a schmear (not of the Pap variety)

☐ ☐ ☐ find a cure for modern ennui

☐ ☐ ☐ poke an anemone

☐ ☐ ☐ ride the tram up to Victoria Peak to see the view of Hong Kong, China

☐ ☐ ☐ take a public stance on the Oxford comma

☐ ☐ ☐ sabre a champagne bottle

☐ ☐ ☐ qualify for an Amex Black Card

☐ ☐ ☐ start a graphic novel book club

☐ ☐ ☐ rub Juliet's boob for luck in Verona, Italy

☐ ☐ ☐ leave an offering for Ganesha

☐ ☐ ☐ fill your keg at a different brewery each week for a year

☐ ☐ ☐ see the Candy Cane Mountains in Azerbaijan

☐ ☐ ☐ embrace the quirkyalone movement

☐ ☐ ☐ catch a fly with chopsticks

☐ ☐ ☐ get dirty in the mud pools at the Totumo Volcano in Colombia

☐ ☐ ☐ serve a three-bird roast

☐ ☐ ☐ listen to K-pop

☐ ☐ ☐ stay in a theme room at the Madonna Inn in San Luis Obispo, California

☐ ☐ ☐ adopt a normcore aesthetic

☐ ☐ ☐ play bicycle polo

☐ ☐ ☐ shop at your local farmers' market

☐ ☐ ☐ go to the Facial Hair Festival in Portland, Maine

☐ ☐ ☐ buy a tagine and make a Moroccan meal

bucket	f*ck it	done it

☐ ☐ ☐ look up at the Burj Khalifa in Dubai, United Arab Emirates

☐ ☐ ☐ eat every shape of pasta at least once

☐ ☐ ☐ align your chakras

☐ ☐ ☐ learn to say "cheers" in five different languages

☐ ☐ ☐ mess with Texas and see what happens

☐ ☐ ☐ island-hop in the Maldives

☐ ☐ ☐ visit an open house just to see how other people live

☐ ☐ ☐ meet a mathlete

☐ ☐ ☐ attain sprezzatura-like ease

☐ ☐ ☐ eat at Yac Donald's in Kagbeni, Nepal

☐ ☐ ☐ guess the exact number of jelly beans in a jar full of jelly beans

☐ ☐ ☐ pray at the "Cinderella High-Heel Church" in Budai Township, Taiwan

☐ ☐ ☐ believe in soup snakes

☐ ☐ ☐ pilgrimage to Prince's Paisley Park
in Minnesota

☐ ☐ ☐ ride in a tuk-tuk

☐ ☐ ☐ create a new font

☐ ☐ ☐ enter the Shitbox Rally in Australia

☐ ☐ ☐ fry an egg on the sidewalk

☐ ☐ ☑ feed a Venus flytrap

☐ ☐ ☐ get over someone by getting under
someone else

☐ ☐ ☐ dip your toes in the Ionian Sea

☐ ☐ ☐ memorise all the allowable two-letter words
before your next Scrabble match

☐ ☐ ☐ high-five *La Mano* sculpture in
Punta del Este, Uruguay

☐ ☐ ☐ cook dinner in a Cowboy Cauldron

☐ ☐ ☐ sip pastis

☐ ☐ ☐ tour the Hash Marihuana & Hemp Museum in Barcelona, Spain

☐ ☐ ☐ make macarons

☐ ☐ ☐ make macaroons

☐ ☐ ☐ explore the Crystal Cave in Bermuda

☐ ☐ ☐ join the American Cheese Society

☐ ☐ ☐ set up a recording studio in your basement

☐ ☐ ☐ work as a mascot

☐ ☐ ☐ use Zener cards to see if you have ESP

☐ ☐ ☐ buy a candy-coloured Vespa

☐ ☐ ☐ meet your doppelgänger

☐ ☐ ☐ plant a Helleborus in your garden and tell everyone it's hella pretty

☐ ☐ ☐ see a Mongolian ovoo

☐ ☐ ☐ teach your parrot to say "I like golden showers"

bucket	f*ck it	done it	
☐	☐	☐	topple a pyramid scheme
☐	☐	☐	search for secret passageways in Bran Castle – resembling the fictional Castle Dracula – in Romania
☐	☐	☐	ask Jay-Z what his 99 problems are
☐	☐	☐	cast an actor to play you in the movie of your life
☐	☐	☐	win a meat raffle
☐	☐	☐	wear a male romper on a first date
☐	☐	☐	speak as fast as an auctioneer
☐	☐	☐	watch the Scripps National Spelling Bee finals
☐	☐	☐	drink banana beer in Rwanda
☐	☐	☐	drink banana wine in the Canary Islands
☐	☐	☐	declare a joint honours degree
☐	☐	☐	witness a frog rain
☐	☐	☐	practise capoeira

☐ ☐ ☐ go Zorbing in New Zealand

☐ ☐ ☐ find the baby in a Mardi Gras king cake

☐ ☐ ☐ tell a lie in Truth or Consequences,
New Mexico

☐ ☐ ☐ beat a lie detector

☐ ☐ ☐ eat *moules-frites* in Belgium

☐ ☐ ☐ ride shotgun in a snowcat making its way up
a mountain

☐ ☐ ☐ forage for fiddleheads

☐ ☐ ☐ strip off at a nudist colony

☐ ☐ ☐ shop at the Feria San Pedro Telmo flea market
in Buenos Aires, Argentina

☐ ☐ ☐ walk a dog for your local animal shelter

☐ ☐ ☐ upgrade your brass knuckles to gold ones

☐ ☐ ☐ wear a fez

☐ ☐ ☐ visit Fez, Morocco

☐ ☐ ☐ sport a waxed moustache

☐ ☐ ☐ stay at the Ice Hotel in Quebec, Canada

☐ ☐ ☐ use a bidet

☐ ☐ ☐ dump someone in front of a love
locks installation

☐ ☐ ☐ hire Wilson Phillips to sing at your wedding

☐ ☐ ☐ cover someone's front garden in pink
plastic flamingos

bucket	f*ck it	done it	
☐	☐	☐	spot land from a ship's crow's nest
☐	☐	☐	incite envy by being both a gourmand and an ectomorph
☐	☐	☐	admire the Bauhaus buildings in the White City of Tel Aviv, Israel
☐	☐	☐	do hot yoga and sweat like a whore in church
☐	☐	☐	pack your lunch in a tiffin carrier
☐	☐	☐	dye your hair pink
☐	☐	☐	start a standing ovation
☐	☐	☐	watch beetle fighting in Laos
☐	☐	☐	play croquet
☐	☐	☐	learn to wiggle your ears
☐	☐	☐	acquire a taste for bitter melon
☐	☐	☐	go razor clamming
☐	☐	☐	get lost in a sea of gingers at the Redhead Days event in the Netherlands

☐ ☐ ☐ hear the cackling call of the kookaburra

☐ ☐ ☐ eat a frankfurter in Frankfurt, Germany

☐ ☐ ☐ read five banned books

☐ ☐ ☐ attend a celebrity roast

☐ ☐ ☐ tour the Tate Britain in London

☐ ☐ ☐ tour the Tate Modern in London

☐ ☐ ☐ make a reservation under the name Mike Hunt

☐ ☐ ☐ shuffle like a dealer

☐ ☐ ☐ find a four-leaf clover

☐ ☐ ☐ compare chocolate and cinnamon babka

☐ ☐ ☐ cross the Charles Bridge in Prague, Czech Republic

☐ ☐ ☐ listen to old radio recordings of Wolfman Jack

☐ ☐ ☐ recognise umami when you taste it

☐ ☐ ☐ pose for stock photos

☐ ☐ ☐ paddle a Vietnamese basket boat

☐ ☐ ☐ host a Monty Python viewing marathon

☐ ☐ ☐ work as a secret shopper

☐ ☐ ☐ slurp raw oysters and see if they make you horny

☐ ☐ ☐ embrace monogamy

☐ ☐ ☐ ride a mechanical bull

☐ ☐ ☐ go glamping

☐ ☐ ☐ scream "This is Sparta" in Sparta, Greece

☐ ☐ ☐ repurpose a coffee table into a shipping pallet

☐ ☐ ☐ find an Easter egg in a movie

☐ ☐ ☐ find an Easter egg in a video game

☐ ☐ ☐ find an Easter egg in a comic book

☐ ☐ ☐ find an Easter egg in a bush

☐ ☐ ☐ watch the stilt fishermen in Sri Lanka

☐ ☐ ☐ settle a dispute with a thumb war

☐ ☐ ☐ try on a suit of armour

☐ ☐ ☐ sip a scotch older than you are

☐ ☐ ☐ embrace polyamory

☐ ☐ ☐ buy a square watermelon in Japan

☐ ☐ ☐ convince someone to vote

☐ ☐ ☐ teach your grandma to fist-bump

☐ ☐ ☐ cage dive with great white sharks

☐ ☐ ☐ visit your old summer camp as an adult

☐ ☐ ☐ ski the perfect bluebird day

☐ ☐ ☐ go to the Malabo International Hip Hop Festival in Equatorial Guinea

☐ ☐ ☐ break a world record

☐ ☐ ☐ consult a seer

☐ ☐ ☐ smash a piñata on the first swing

☐ ☐ ☐ enter a belly flop competition

☐ ☐ ☐ people-watch at Chateau Marmont in
Los Angeles, California

☐ ☐ ☐ buy, renovate, and sell a house

☐ ☐ ☐ mime

☐ ☐ ☐ hustle someone at pool

☐ ☐ ☐ disregard Murphy's Law

☐ ☐ ☐ soak in a claw-foot tub

☐ ☐ ☐ build a bonfire on
Bonfire Night

☐ ☐ ☐ see the Brighton bathing boxes in
Melbourne, Australia

☐ ☐ ☐ plant a guerrilla garden

☐ ☐ ☐ give out *lai see* for Chinese New Year

☐ ☐ ☐ observe Earth Hour

15

bucket
f*ck it
done it

☐ ☐ ☐ walk down the green sand Papakōlea Beach in Hawaii

☐ ☐ ☐ climb a *via ferrata*

☐ ☐ ☐ eat *pintxos* in San Sebastián, Spain

☐ ☐ ☐ perfect your Blue Steel pose

☐ ☐ ☐ organise an adult prom

☐ ☐ ☐ hug Amma, the spiritual leader

☐ ☐ ☐ ride a vintage carousel

☐ ☐ ☐ stand at the edge of Pulpit Rock in Norway

☐ ☐ ☐ date a blerd

☐ ☐ ☐ wear a green carnation on your lapel like Oscar Wilde

☐ ☐ ☐ storm watch in Tofino, Canada

☐ ☐ ☐ invent a third kind of clam chowder that is better than Manhattan and New England

☐ ☐ ☐ play the Pink Panther song on the saxophone

☐ ☐ ☐ play the Snoopy song on the piano

□ □ □ make a kitten watch YouTube videos of humans doing cute things

□ □ □ drive a Zamboni

□ □ □ blindfold a wine snob and do a taste test

□ □ □ go an entire summer without getting a brain freeze

□ □ □ ditch Tinder and head to the Lisdoonvarna Matchmaking Festival in Ireland

□ □ □ watch all of Jean-Luc Godard's films

□ □ □ bang a gong

□ □ □ convince someone that a ménage à trois is a vigorous bout of spring cleaning

□ □ □ float alongside a Moorish idol while snorkelling

□ □ □ listen to all of the Live at Budokan albums

□ □ □ fire a T-shirt cannon into a crowd

□ □ □ see Boiling Lake in Dominica

bucket it
f*ck it
done it

☐ ☐ ☐ see Boiling River in Peru

☐ ☐ ☐ cook with ghee

☐ ☐ ☐ learn the difference between
liqueur and eau-de-vie

☐ ☐ ☐ fish for crappie

☐ ☐ ☐ learn an idiot-proof magic trick

☐ ☐ ☐ compare Montreal and New York bagels
and pick a favourite

☐ ☐ ☐ stand on the equator

☐ ☐ ☐ greet someone with a Corleone-style
cheek pinch

☐ ☐ ☐ quote Joseph Campbell

☐ ☐ ☐ watch Turkish oil wrestling in Istanbul, Turkey

☐ ☐ ☐ hang out in an old honky-tonk

☐ ☐ ☐ find a crop circle

☐ ☐ ☐ ask yourself, "What would Joan Jett do?"

☐ ☐ ☐ chew on a salty *dubbel zout*

☐ ☐ ☐ celebrate with a round of picklebacks instead of champagne

☐ ☐ ☐ take pictures from the observation deck of the Oriental Pearl Tower in Shanghai, China

☐ ☐ ☐ help preserve Haiti's gingerbread houses

☐ ☐ ☐ cover your bed with money and roll around on it

☐ ☐ ☐ gaze at your reflection in the *Cloud Gate* sculpture in Chicago, Illinois

☐ ☐ ☐ speak with a fake accent for a day

☐ ☐ ☐ toss pizza dough like a pro

☐ ☐ ☐ sleep on a portaledge

☐ ☐ ☐ meet an ecosexual

☐ ☐ ☐ bag munros in Scotland

☐ ☐ ☐ infiltrate the Bearded Villains and see what happens

☐ ☐ ☐ smear *thanakha* paste on your face in Myanmar

☐ ☐ ☐ make a Mountain Dew cake

☐ ☐ ☐ see a Jesus Christ lizard run on water

☐ ☐ ☐ honk before driving into a tunnel
to ward off evil spirits

☐ ☐ ☐ eat Roquefort cheese in
Roquefort, France

☐ ☐ ☐ adopt a French bulldog

☐ ☐ ☐ win a Webby Award

☐ ☐ ☐ take your frustration out on a Whac-A-Mole

☐ ☐ ☐ watch the Mermaid Parade in Coney Island,
New York

☐ ☐ ☐ carry a good luck charm

☐ ☐ ☐ buy carbon offsets each time you fly

☐ ☐ ☐ overhear someone call you a MILF

☐ ☐ ☐ hike along the *levadas* in Madeira, Portugal

☐ ☐ ☐ hood slide like Bo Duke

☐ ☐ ☐ practise Brazilian jiujitsu

☐ ☐ ☐ read about yawning
without yawning

☐ ☐ ☐ pose nude for
Spencer Tunick

☐ ☐ ☐ go leaf peeping in New England

☐ ☐ ☐ sleep on a waterbed

☐ ☐ ☐ read all of Haruki Murakami's books

☐ ☐ ☐ assume the silly mid-off position on a
cricket team

☐ ☐ ☐ release a sky lantern at the Lantern Festival in
Taipei, Taiwan

☐ ☐ ☐ walk on your hands

☐ ☐ ☐ sing sea shanties

☐ ☐ ☐ heed Coco Chanel's advice and take one
thing off before you walk out the door

☐ ☐ ☐ eat *fartons* in Valencia, Spain

☐ ☐ ☐ run a four-minute mile

☐ ☐ ☐ direct a music video

bucket
f*ck it
done it

☐ ☐ ☐ learn to speak Esperanto

☐ ☐ ☐ moonlight as a ventriloquist

☐ ☐ ☐ watch a camel race in Qatar

☐ ☐ ☐ celebrate International Masturbation Day

☐ ☐ ☐ hop on a cable car in San Francisco, California

☐ ☐ ☐ test-drive an Aston Martin

☐ ☐ ☐ build a half-pipe in your backyard

☐ ☐ ☐ visit the Cats Museum in Kotor, Montenegro

☐ ☐ ☐ shop at a haberdashery

☐ ☐ ☐ carry a handkerchief

☐ ☐ ☐ sweat it out in a Mayan *temazcal*

☐ ☐ ☐ play frolf

☐ ☐ ☐ go to a Fighting Cholitas wrestling match in El Alto, Bolivia

☐ ☐ ☐ ride in a sidecar

☐ ☐ ☐ eat a lobster roll in Maine

☐ ☐ ☐ successfully elude a stage five clinger

☐ ☐ ☐ rap your wedding vows

☐ ☐ ☐ keep the hotel bathrobe

☐ ☐ ☐ hold a piece of the Berlin Wall in your hand

☐ ☐ ☐ watch every episode of *The Golden Girls*

☐ ☐ ☐ drop £20 in a busker's hat

☐ ☐ ☐ write to an agony aunt and see your letter printed

☐ ☐ ☐ browse a seed catalogue

bucket	f*ck it	done it	
☐	☐	☐	attend a Japanese tea ceremony
☐	☐	☐	attend an Ethiopian coffee ceremony
☐	☐	☐	jump on a bed at a five-star hotel
☐	☐	☐	bribe a bouncer to bypass the line
☐	☐	☐	put your wit to use and start a greetings card company
☐	☐	☐	meet Senhor Testiculo, the Brazilian testicular cancer mascot
☐	☐	☐	sport a pompadour
☐	☐	☐	join Mensa
☐	☐	☐	taste cactus marmalade
☐	☐	☐	visit the Guggenheim in New York, Bilbao, Venice and Abu Dhabi
☐	☐	☐	apply for a Guggenheim Fellowship
☐	☐	☐	launch a catapult

☐ ☐ ☐ travel the length of an isthmus

☐ ☐ ☐ make beer can chicken

☐ ☐ ☐ drink a Singapore Sling at Raffles Singapore

☐ ☐ ☐ portage a canoe

☐ ☐ ☐ start a conga line

☐ ☐ ☐ identify as a flâneur

☐ ☐ ☐ ask Prince Albert of Monaco if he has a
Prince Albert piercing

☐ ☐ ☐ wear a nun's habit to see if you are
treated differently

☐ ☐ ☐ stay in a houseboat on Dal Lake in
Kashmir, India

☐ ☐ ☐ find your muse

☐ ☐ ☐ sit on a giant Adirondack chair

☐ ☐ ☐ watch a dog while it's dreaming

☐ ☐ ☐ go to a Full Moon Party in Thailand

☐ ☐ ☐ take a pole dancing class

☐ ☐ ☐ come up with a thousand words to describe one picture

☐ ☐ ☐ see an oasis in the desert

☐ ☐ ☐ celebrate Kwanzaa

☐ ☐ ☐ compose a haiku

☐ ☐ ☐ ride in a hunter/jumper competition

☐ ☐ ☐ hire a virtual assistant

☐ ☐ ☐ soak in the Blue Lagoon in Iceland

IF I MEET OPRAH
I WILL DIE FROM HER GREATNESS
IT WILL BE WORTH IT.

☐ ☐ ☐ spend time in a matriarchal society

☐ ☐ ☐ Jelly wrestle

☐ ☐ ☐ order blini and caviar at Café Pushkin in Moscow, Russia

☐ ☐ ☐ feed the swimming pigs on Big Major Cay in the Bahamas

☐ ☐ ☐ run and drink with the Hash House Harriers

☐ ☐ ☐ live on a kibbutz

☐ ☐ ☐ sit in a salt cave

☐ ☐ ☐ walk on stilts

☐ ☐ ☐ watch a teppanyaki chef in action

☐ ☐ ☐ eat bunny chow in Durban, South Africa

☐ ☐ ☐ rake the sand in a Zen garden

☐ ☐ ☐ pose for a pic with the *Fremont Troll* sculpture in Seattle, Washington

☐ ☐ ☐ memorise a Pablo Neruda poem and recite it to your love

☐ ☐ ☐ escape an escape room

☐ ☐ ☐ shop at a German Christmas market

☐ ☐ ☐ study anti-art

☐ ☐ ☐ drive across the Bixby Bridge in Big Sur, California

☐ ☐ ☐ indulge in a gratuitous guitar solo

☐ ☐ ☐ try vaginal steaming

☐ ☐ ☐ watch a game of murderball

☐ ☐ ☐ collect all of R. Crumb's comics

☐ ☐ ☐ eat a smoked meat sandwich at Schwartz's Deli in Montreal, Canada

☐ ☐ ☐ see a rainbow eucalyptus tree in Hawaii

☐ ☐ ☐ only buy dresses with pockets

☐ ☐ ☐ frequent your local library

☐ ☐ ☐ open an Etsy store

☐ ☐ ☐ see a pink moon

☐ ☐ ☐ go bog snorkelling in Wales

☐ ☐ ☐ quote Dorothy Parker

☐ ☐ ☐ buy a vintage Gunne Sax dress

☐ ☐ ☐ adopt a steampunk aesthetic

☐ ☐ ☐ do the splits like Jean-Claude
Van Damme

#1
BELIEBER

☐ ☐ ☐ get a hand-poked tattoo

☐ ☐ ☐ get a tramp stamp

☐ ☐ ☐ get your tramp stamp lasered off

☐ ☐ ☐ greet someone with a French *bise*

☐ ☐ ☐ practise Transcendental Meditation

☐ ☐ ☐ look up at the *gallarija* balconies in
Valletta, Malta

☐ ☐ ☐ make sun tea

☐ ☐ ☐ swim in the Atlantic Ocean and Caribbean
Sea on the same day

☐ ☐ ☐ visit Taumatawhakatangihangakoauauotama-
teaturipukakapikimaungahoronukupokaiwhenu-
akitanatahu in New Zealand

☐ ☐ ☐ use a monocle instead of
wearing glasses

☐ ☐ ☐ listen to every episode of
This American Life on NPR

☐ ☐ ☐ drink Butterbeer

☐ ☐ ☐ shave with a straight razor

☐ ☐ ☐ ride a funicular in Valparaíso, Chile

☐ ☐ ☐ crowd-surf

☐ ☐ ☐ invent a new drinking game

☐ ☐ ☐ see the cliff villages in the Bandiagara
Escarpment of Mali

☐ ☐ ☐ watch all of the James Bond movies

☐ ☐ ☐ experience lucid dreaming

☐ ☐ ☐ root for the anti-hero

☐ ☐ ☐ meet a Brony

bucket	f*ck it	done it	
☐	☐	☐	scour a garage sale for undiscovered treasures
☐	☐	☐	walk somewhere backwards
☐	☐	☐	buy an original Shepard Fairey piece
☐	☐	☐	eat at a trattoria, *ristorante*, osteria, pizzeria, *enoteca*, *pasticceria*, and *gelateria* in Italy
☐	☐	☐	swing a mace
☐	☐	☐	refer to something as "slicker than deer guts on a doorknob"
☐	☐	☐	enter a chilli cook-off
☐	☐	☐	bury a time capsule
☐	☐	☐	surf in Biarritz, France
☐	☐	☐	play Six Degrees of Kevin Bacon
☐	☐	☐	take the Tube and mind the gap
☐	☐	☐	watch La Quebrada Cliff Divers in Acapulco, Mexico
☐	☐	☐	wear a Canadian tuxedo
☐	☐	☐	go gunkholing

☑ ☐ ☐ see the aurora borealis

☐ ☐ ☐ ride a unicycle

☐ ☐ ☐ see the Stanley Cup
but don't touch it

☑ ☐ ☐ splash around in a
public fountain

☐ ☐ ☐ explore Freetown
Christiania in
Copenhagen, Denmark

☐ ☐ ☐ drink blue Clitoria tea

☐ ☐ ☐ demand an inclusion rider

☐ ☐ ☐ get caked at a Steve Aoki show

☑ ☐ ☐ dip your toes in the Black Sea

☐ ☐ ☐ take the Star Ferry from Hong Kong Island
to Kowloon, China

☐ ☐ ☐ bin dive

☐ ☐ ☐ sleep in a yurt

☐ ☐ ☐ buy nothing on Buy Nothing Day

☐ ☐ ☐ meet an Elvis impersonator

☐ ☐ ☐ share a pupu platter in Hawaii

☐ ☐ ☐ hug a boabob tree

☐ ☐ ☐ stomp grapes at a winery

☐ ☐ ☐ get dirty at La Tomatina in Buñol, Spain

☐ ☐ ☑ solve a Rubik's Cube

☐ ☐ ☐ enter a speedcubing competition

☐ ☐ ☑ ask someone to draw you like one of their French girls

☐ ☐ ☐ visit the town of Muff, Ireland

☐ ☐ ☐ watch millions of bats fly out from under the Congress Avenue Bridge in Austin, Texas

☐ ☐ ☐ dedicate a song to someone on the radio

☐ ☐ ☐ prove definitively that it is good luck when a bird shits on you

☐ ☐ ☐ play at the high rollers table

☐ ☐ ☐ look up at the giant Moai on Easter Island

bucket
f*ck it
done it

☐ ☐ ☐ learn to wrap a sari

☐ ☐ ☐ fill up your passport

☐ ☐ ☐ ogle the erotic sculptures in Khajuraho, India

☐ ☐ ☐ solve an acrostic

☐ ☐ ☐ go on a silent retreat

☐ ☐ ☐ learn to love Vegemite

☐ ☐ ☐ complete NaNoWriMo

☐ ☐ ☐ prepare thoughtfully for a zombie apocalypse

☐ ☐ ☐ fill your pockets with catnip and visit Cat Island in Japan

☐ ☐ ☐ watch all of Sofia Coppola's movies

☐ ☐ ☐ figure out which number you are on the Kinsey Scale

☐ ☐ ☐ watch a horror movie on Valentine's Day

34

☐ ☐ ☐   collect Hawaiian shirts

☐ ☐ ☐   discover a
secret wall tattoo
behind a painting in
your hotel room

☐ ☐ ☐   eat a po'boy in New
Orleans, Louisiana

☐ ☐ ☐   get cosy in a Cowichan sweater

☐ ☐ ☐   sub your regular sub for a banh mi

☐ ☐ ☐   throw out the ceremonial first pitch at a
baseball game

☐ ☐ ☐   stay at the Pantone Hotel in Brussels, Belgium

☐ ☐ ☐   sneeze with your eyes open

☐ ☐ ☐   drink absinthe

☐ ☐ ☐   island-hop in Micronesia

☐ ☐ ☐   screw life coaching and trust your gut

☐ ☐ ☐   wear a loincloth

☐ ☐ ☐   cross the international date line

☐ ☐ ☐ take the scenic route along Clarence Drive in South Africa

☐ ☐ ☐ find parallels between *The Big Lebowski* and *The Myth of Sisyphus*

☐ ☐ ☐ recreate the *Kiss by the Hôtel de Ville* photograph

☐ ☐ ☐ join a Theatresports team

☐ ☐ ☐ admire the street art in George Town, Malaysia

☐ ☐ ☐ host a fondue party

☐ ☐ ☐ play the ukulele

☐ ☐ ☐ spelunk

☐ ☐ ☐ eat a meal so spicy you sweat through your shirt

☐ ☐ ☐ stay at the Wigwam Motel in Holbrook, Arizona

☐ ☐ ☐ go ice fishing

☐ ☐ ☐ sport an afro

bucket	*f*ck it*	*done it*

☐ ☐ ☐ try tightlacing

☐ ☐ ☐ study Norse mythology

☐ ☐ ☐ listen to a steel pan band in Trinidad

☐ ☐ ☐ support the Free the Nipple campaign

☐ ☐ ☐ circumnavigate an island on a Jet Ski

☐ ☐ ☐ stuff your own sausage

☐ ☐ ☐ people-watch from a café overlooking the Piazza del Campo in Siena, Italy

☐ ☐ ☐ beatbox

☐ ☐ ☐ put a worry doll under your pillow

☐ ☐ ☐ burn some sage to purify your space

☐ ☐ ☐ hold a Grammy in your hands

☐ ☐ ☐ paddle a dragon boat

☐ ☐ ☐ add your Brownie badges to your CV

☐ ☐ ☐ stay at an ashram

BEST POLKA ALBUM

☐ ☐ ☐ carry the Olympic torch

☐ ☐ ☐ win a "Master of Your Domain" contest

☐ ☐ ☐ party at the Pink Palace in Corfu, Greece

☐ ☐ ☐ get out of the friend zone

☐ ☐ ☐ have an epiphany

☐ ☐ ☐ shop at a souk

☐ ☐ ☐ read all of Joan Didion's books

☐ ☐ ☐ bite bravely into a thousand-year-old egg

☐ ☐ ☐ stay at the Stanley Hotel in Colorado – which inspired Stephen King's *The Shining*

☐ ☐ ☐ pack your lunch in an aeroplane sick bag so no one steals it

☐ ☐ ☐ meet a bona fide Canadian hoser

☐ ☐ ☐ meet a bona fide chav

bucket
f*ck it
done it

☐ ☐ ☐ play swamp soccer in Finland

☐ ☐ ☐ find out how many Altoids you can put in your mouth at once

☐ ☐ ☐ spin a dreidel

☐ ☐ ☐ cut your way through the jungle with a machete

☐ ☐ ☐ pet an alpaca without being spat on

☐ ☐ ☐ see an emerald sunset in Jericoacoara, Brazil

☐ ☐ ☐ get your handwriting analysed

☐ ☐ ☐ drive a lowrider down Whittier Boulevard in East Los Angeles, California

☐ ☐ ☐ try laughter yoga

☐ ☐ ☐ celebrate Diwali

☐ ☐ ☐ regale a fellow raconteur

☐ ☐ ☐ get a feel for the town of Brest in Belarus

☐ ☐ ☐ listen to a throat singer

☐ ☐ ☐ ferment your own kimchi

☐ ☐ ☐ master barefoot waterskiing

☐ ☐ ☐ swim in the bioluminescent bay in Vieques, Puerto Rico

☐ ☐ ☐ write a palindromic sentence

☐ ☐ ☐ enrol at Harvard

☐ ☐ ☐ create an app

☐ ☐ ☐ run Rocky-style up the steps of the Philadelphia Museum of Art

☐ ☐ ☐ drink aquavit in Sweden

☐ ☐ ☐ tuck a hibiscus in your hair

☐ ☐ ☐ dress like Stevie Nicks circa *Rumours*

☐ ☐ ☐ watch ten movies that pass the Bechdel Test

☐ ☐ ☐ buy a Philippe Starck Louis Ghost chair

☐ ☐ ☐ experience déjà vu

☐ ☐ ☐ experience *jamais vu*

☐ ☐ ☐ experience *déjà rêvé*

☐ ☐ ☐ take the world's shortest flight (two minutes) in the Orkney Islands

☐ ☐ ☐ stroll through Forsyth Park in Savannah, Georgia

☐ ☐ ☐ add the words "in bed" to the end of your fortune cookie fortune

☐ ☐ ☐ make marshmallows from scratch

☐ ☐ ☐ compare scars with someone – physical or otherwise

☐ ☐ ☐ work as an extra in a Hollywood film

☐ ☐ ☐ work as an extra in a Bollywood film

☐ ☐ ☐ work as an extra in a Nollywood film

☐ ☐ ☐ go mudding in a 4x4

☐ ☐ ☐ see the *Child Eater of Bern* statue in Switzerland

☐ ☐ ☐ sidle up to your crush under the mistletoe

☐ ☐ ☐ meet a fruitarian

☐ ☐ ☐ turn up the heat, make blended drinks, and pretend you're on vacation

☐ ☐ ☐ lie on Maho Beach in Saint Martin as a plane flies over

☐ ☐ ☐ leave an offering for the holy rodents at the Temple of Rats in Rajasthan, India

☐ ☐ ☐ soak in the hot springs on Margaret Island, Hungary

☐ ☐ ☐ take up beekeeping

☐ ☐ ☐ join the mile-high club

☐ ☐ ☐ do a one-arm push-up

☐ ☐ ☐ experience déjà vu

☐ ☐ ☐ join a Jane's Walk in your city

☐ ☐ ☐ dive from the Stari Most Bridge in Mostar, Bosnia and Herzegovina

☐ ☐ ☐ get wet at a Songkran water fight in Thailand

☐ ☐ ☐ go on a news fast

☐ ☐ ☐ design jewellery

☐ ☐ ☐ lick a psychoactive toad
and get high

☐ ☐ ☐ stay at a capsule hotel
in Tokyo, Japan

☐ ☐ ☐ wear Speedos
with confidence

☐ ☐ ☐ ride in a blimp

☐ ☐ ☐ put a down payment on a house with the
contents of your swear jar

☐ ☐ ☐ leave a guitar pick on Jimi Hendrix's grave

☐ ☐ ☐ visit Stonehenge in Wiltshire

☐ ☐ ☐ understand the Danish concept of *hygge*

☐ ☐ ☐ hire a midwife instead of a doctor

☐ ☐ ☐ watch *The Wizard of Oz* while playing Pink
Floyd's *The Dark Side of the Moon* and see if
they sync up

☐ ☐ ☐ win a wishbone pull

☐ ☐ ☐ earn your black belt

bucket f*ck it done it

- [ ] [ ] [ ] buy a box of Voodoo Doughnuts in Portland, Oregon
- [ ] [ ] [ ] study Jungian dream interpretation
- [ ] [ ] [ ] collect PEZ dispensers
- [ ] [ ] [ ] hit someone with a plastic hammer at the Festa de São João in Portugal
- [ ] [ ] [ ] be carried in a sedan chair
- [ ] [ ] [ ] read the Bhagavad Gita
- [ ] [ ] [ ] watch all of David Lynch's movies
- [ ] [ ] [ ] go to a poetry slam
- [ ] [ ] [ ] wear rose-coloured glasses literally
- [ ] [ ] [ ] wear rose-coloured glasses metaphorically
- [ ] [ ] [ ] pedal around a velodrome
- [ ] [ ] [ ] drink a daiquiri at El Floridita in Havana, Cuba
- [ ] [ ] [ ] give yourself a coffee enema
- [ ] [ ] [ ] play a didgeridoo

☐ ☐ ☐ email Perez Hilton with a tip that breaks a
huge story

☐ ☐ ☐ walk around the Plain of Jars in
Phonsavan, Laos

☐ ☐ ☐ refuse to plan your life around
Mercury retrograde

☐ ☐ ☐ eat fried green tomatoes

☐ ☐ ☐ ogle the displays at the Phallological Museum
in Iceland

☐ ☐ ☐ find the town of Clit, Romania

☐ ☐ ☐ learn to love haggis

☐ ☐ ☐ meet Banksy

☐ ☐ ☐ try extreme couponing

☐ ☐ ☐ eat at a roadside jerk stand in Jamaica

☐ ☐ ☐ see Halley's Comet

☐ ☐ ☐ disavow the five-second rule

☐ ☐ ☐ hang out in Dude Chilling Park in
Vancouver, Canada

80% OFF
UPPER LIP WAXING

☐ ☐ ☐ go to a midnight screening of *The Rocky Horror Picture Show*

☐ ☐ ☐ watch a male seahorse give birth

☐ ☐ ☐ buy vinyl on International Record Store Day

☐ ☐ ☐ yodel

☐ ☐ ☐ high-five a random toddler

☐ ☐ ☐ stay at a *riad* in Marrakech, Morocco

☐ ☐ ☐ indulge in a lomilomi massage

☐ ☐ ☐ taste camel's milk chocolate

☐ ☐ ☐ swim in a cenote

☐ ☐ ☐ spot the mysterious lights in Marfa, Texas

☐ ☐ ☐ fly first-class

☐ ☐ ☐ get drunk in a tiki bar

☐ ☐ ☐ consult a medical intuitive

☐ ☐ ☐ adopt a courtesy title

☐ ☐ ☐ relax in an infrared sauna

☐ ☐ ☐ see the pink Lake Retba in Senegal

☐ ☐ ☐ see the pink Lake Hillier in Australia

☐ ☐ ☐ belly dance

☐ ☐ ☐ watch piranhas being fed

☐ ☐ ☐ attend the BET Awards

☐ ☐ ☐ kiss your partner at the end of the
Pärnu Seawall in Estonia

☐ ☐ ☐ describe something
as Kafkaesque

☐ ☐ ☐ reenact the
Dirty Dancing
lift with your dog

☐ ☐ ☐ find out what was in
Marsellus Wallace's
briefcase in *Pulp Fiction*

☐ ☐ ☐ join a Roller Derby team

☐ ☐ ☐ start a synth-pop band

☐ ☐ ☐ enter the Empire State Building Run-Up in
New York, New York

☐ ☐ ☐ shave your head

☐ ☐ ☐ bathe a goat during the San Juan Festival in Tenerife, Canary Islands

☐ ☐ ☐ pimp your ride

☐ ☐ ☐ have sex under a mosquito net in an exotic locale

☐ ☐ ☐ lower a drawbridge over a moat

☐ ☐ ☐ spin poi

☐ ☐ ☐ visit the Chemosphere House in Los Angeles, California

☐ ☐ ☐ mountain bike down Bolivia's Road of Death

☐ ☐ ☐ relax in a flotation tank

☐ ☐ ☐ grow your own wheatgrass

☐ ☐ ☐ wakeboard

☐ ☐ ☐ go to an open casting call

☐ ☐ ☐ familiarise yourself with Fibonacci numbers

☐ ☐ ☐ visit the Rainbow Village in Taiwan

bucket
f*ck it
done it

☐ ☐ ☐ hang a pair of panties on the ceiling at the
Panty Bar in Paternoster, South Africa

☐ ☐ ☐ do an aerial cartwheel

☐ ☐ ☐ listen to Edith Piaf and pretend
you're in Paris, France

☐ ☐ ☐ hypnotise a chicken

☐ ☐ ☐ stay at an eco-resort

☐ ☐ ☐ find a vintage couture gown in a charity shop

☐ ☐ ☐ agree that red velvet cake is played out and
eat it anyway

☐ ☐ ☐ walk the length of Hadrian's Wall

☐ ☐ ☐ memorise all the words to every song
in *Grease*

☐ ☐ ☐ experience synesthesia

☐ ☐ ☐ join the Church of the Flying Spaghetti
Monster as a pastafarian

☐ ☐ ☐ drive a biodiesel car

☐ ☐ ☐ watch a whirling dervish

☐ ☐ ☐ ride in a swan boat in the Public Garden in Boston, Massachusetts

☐ ☐ ☐ ride shotgun in a monster truck

☐ ☐ ☐ write fan fiction

☐ ☐ ☐ eat astronaut ice cream

☐ ☐ ☐ see the Devil's Town rock formations in Serbia

☐ ☐ ☐ quote Langston Hughes

☐ ☐ ☐ poach a piece of fish in your dishwasher

☐ ☐ ☐ go coasteering in Wales

☐ ☐ ☐ catch a pop fly playing baseball

☐ ☐ ☐ eat an Oreo before going to the dentist

☐ ☐ ☐ dive down to the underwater post office in Mele Bay, Vanuatu

☐ ☐ ☐ use an antique typewriter

☐ ☐ ☐ manage to make offal taste good

☐ ☐ ☐ manscape religiously

☐ ☐ ☐ volunteer for Big Brothers/Big Sisters
of America

☐ ☐ ☐ celebrate Cinco de Mayo sans cheap tequila
and sombrero

☐ ☐ ☐ get dirty at the Boryeong Mud Festival in
Seoul, South Korea

☐ ☐ ☐ argue with a sophist

☐ ☐ ☐ play the banjo

☐ ☐ ☐ curl at a bonspiel

☐ ☐ ☐ go on an airboat tour of the Everglades
in Florida

☐ ☐ ☐ see a Komodo dragon in Indonesia

☐ ☐ ☐ compete in a pumpkin regatta

☐ ☐ ☐ foster an interest in genealogy and fill in your
family tree

☐ ☐ ☐ convince someone that Joan of Arc was
Noah's wife

☐ ☐ ☐ peel an apple in one long continuous strand

☐ ☐ ☐ travel faster than the speed of sound

☐ ☐ ☐ eat yak jerky in Tibet

☐ ☐ ☐ compose a homage to the 80s with
a synthesiser

☐ ☐ ☐ compare Yves Klein Blue and Majorelle Blue
and pick a favourite

☐ ☐ ☐ attend a Renaissance Fair

☐ ☐ ☐ punt down a lazy river

☐ ☐ ☐ dabble in Dionysian-style debauchery in the
Greek Islands

☐ ☐ ☐ brew your own beer

☐ ☐ ☐ slackline

☐ ☐ ☐ graduate from slacklining to highlining

☐ ☐ ☐ backpack around Southeast Asia

☐ ☐ ☐ buy a Rolex

☐ ☐ ☐ tell someone that they "had you at hello"

☐ ☐ ☐ go to Mawsynram, India — the wettest place on earth

☐ ☐ ☐ go to the Atacama Desert, in Chile — the driest place on earth

☐ ☐ ☐ get table service in a club

☐ ☐ ☐ hit the bull's-eye on a dartboard

☐ ☐ ☐ trick someone into drinking wiener water

☐ ☐ ☐ wear a tiara

☐ ☐ ☐ admire the art deco architecture in Detroit, Michigan

☐ ☐ ☐ try a different cheese every week for a year

☐ ☐ ☐ write erotica

☐ ☐ ☐ bend it like Beckham

☐ ☐ ☐ do your makeup to mimic the Eye of Horus

☐☐☐ visit Frida Kahlo's house in Mexico City, Mexico

☐☐☐ play mahjongg

☐☐☐ meet a gaucho

☐☐☐ hire a caterer and take all the credit

MUSEO FRIDA KAHLO

☐☐☐ shadowbox

☐☐☐ find a fossil

☐☐☐ drive across the Bosphorus Bridge in Istanbul, Turkey

☐☐☐ visit all of Rem Koolhaas's buildings

☐☐☐ eat a vagina-shaped *karjalanpiirakka* pastry in Helsinki, Finland

☐☐☐ host your own cooking show

☐☐☐ have the house with the most Christmas lights on your street

☐☐☐ read all of the gravestones in a pet cemetery

☐ ☐ ☐ take pictures during the golden hour

☐ ☐ ☐ ice-skate on Rideau Canal in Ottawa, Canada

☐ ☐ ☐ swing from a trapeze

☐ ☐ ☐ witness an Umbanda ritual

☐ ☐ ☐ embrace the stride of pride instead of the walk of shame

☐ ☐ ☐ open your third eye

☐ ☐ ☐ drink Masala Coke in India

☐ ☐ ☐ drink Inca Kola in Peru

☐ ☐ ☐ drink Corsica Cola in Corsica, France

☐ ☐ ☐ wear a kimono

☐ ☐ ☐ subscribe to all of your favourite magazines

☐ ☐ ☐ get invited to a pig pickin'

☐ ☐ ☐ see the female Led Zeppelin tribute band Lez Zeppelin in concert

☐ ☐ ☐ enter your hot rod in a show and shine

☐ ☐ ☐ find a cure for xanthophobia

☐ ☐ ☐ climb Jacob's Ladder in Jamestown, Saint Helena

☐ ☐ ☐ slice a persimmon seed in half and predict the weather for the upcoming winter

☐ ☐ ☐ explore the Mayan ruins in Copan, Honduras

☐ ☐ ☐ spread the gospel of shower beers

☐ ☐ ☐ paint like Pollock

☐ ☐ ☐ tie a bow tie

☐ ☐ ☐ light a candle at a shrine for Jesús Malverde in Mexico

☐ ☐ ☐ cut a ceremonial ribbon

☐ ☐ ☐ cook a green curry

☐ ☐ ☐ cook a red curry

☐ ☐ ☐ cook a yellow curry

☐ ☐ ☐ find a cure for anatidaephobia

☐ ☐ ☐ pilgrimage to Bob Marley's house in Nine Mile, Jamaica

☐ ☐ ☐ learn to speak Portuguese

☐ ☐ ☐ yell "bravo" at the end of a performance

☐ ☐ ☐ play Donkey Kong on the original Nintendo

☐ ☐ ☐ visit the town of Llabià, Spain

☐ ☐ ☐ refer to noodles as "long-ass rice"

☐ ☐ ☐ use an ulu instead of a knife

☐ ☐ ☐ people-watch at the arrivals gate at the airport

☐ ☐ ☐ see the wild parrots in San Francisco, California

☐ ☐ ☐ kick a field goal

☐ ☐ ☐ drink turnip wine

☐ ☐ ☐ learn to love durian

☐ ☐ ☐ admire the Zanzibar doors in Stone Town, Tanzania

SUPER FINE TURNIP WINE

bucket
f*ck it
done it

☐ ☐ ☐ host a yearly Oscars party

☐ ☐ ☐ pay someone to put on your duvet cover

☐ ☐ ☐ watch the X Games

☐ ☐ ☐ make borscht without it looking like you murdered someone in your kitchen

☐ ☐ ☐ use "banana" as your safety word

☐ ☐ ☐ shop at a sample sale

☐ ☐ ☐ earn a *compostela* for completing the El Camino de Santiago pilgrimage

☐ ☐ ☐ refuse to refer to trail mix as gorp

☐ ☐ ☐ scuba dive Belize's Great Blue Hole

☐ ☐ ☐ fold one thousand origami cranes and make a wish

☐ ☐ ☐ cross the skybridge at the Petronas Twin Towers in Kuala Lumpur, Malaysia

☐ ☐ ☐ play the keytar

☐ ☐ ☐ jump on the bandwagon

bucket	**f*ck it**	**done it**	

□ □ □ achieve the perfect cereal/milk ratio on the first pour

□ □ □ bleach your hair

□ □ □ spot a humuhumunukunukuapua'a in Hawaiian waters

□ □ □ witness an exorcism

□ □ □ affix a set of horns to the front of your car

□ □ □ eat jellied eels in the East End

□ □ □ perfect your poker face

□ □ □ mosh

□ □ □ read rune stones

□ □ □ feed the pigeons in Saint Mark's Square in Venice, Italy

□ □ □ lie on a bed of nails

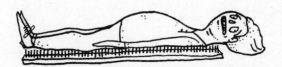

☐ ☐ ☐ join your pet for a nap in a sunny spot

☐ ☐ ☐ climb a coconut tree in your bare feet

☐ ☐ ☐ marry for love

☐ ☐ ☐ marry for money

☐ ☐ ☐ marry for citizenship

☐ ☐ ☐ wear lederhosen

☐ ☐ ☐ explore the tunnels under the Bock
         in Luxembourg

☐ ☐ ☐ buy a loaf of Poilâne bread in Paris

☐ ☐ ☐ come in extra hot for a handshake to
         assert dominance

☐ ☐ ☐ consult a fortune-teller at the Temple Street
         Night Market in Hong Kong, China

☐ ☐ ☐ write your name in wet cement

☐ ☐ ☐ flex at Muscle Beach in Venice, California

☐ ☐ ☐ see an *inuksuk*

☐ ☐ ☐ alter your consciousness with binaural beats

	bucket	f*ck it	done it

☐ ☐ ☐ date a gymnast

☐ ☐ ☐ soak in the hot springs in Salto, Uruguay

☐ ☐ ☐ smell the semen-scented Callery pear tree
as it blooms

☐ ☐ ☐ watch a duelling pianos performance

☐ ☐ ☐ take part in the Running of the Boots in
Sitka, Alaska

☐ ☐ ☐ try birch syrup instead of maple

☐ ☐ ☐ quote Dolly Parton

☐ ☐ ☐ embrace your cankles

☐ ☐ ☐ cruise the Nile

☐ ☐ ☐ greet someone at the airport
with a giant sign

☐ ☐ ☐ crush a Polo and see if it sparks

☐ ☐ ☐ summit Mount Ramelau in
East Timor

☐ ☐ ☐ use the placebo effect to your advantage

M. CAREY

61

☐ ☐ ☐ swing dance

☐ ☐ ☐ adopt two lovebirds and name them after your favourite celebrity couple

☐ ☐ ☐ wear full KISS makeup to a KISS concert

☐ ☐ ☐ go to a finger-pulling competition at the Arctic Winter Games in Greenland

☐ ☐ ☐ fill your wine rack with Lambrini

☐ ☐ ☐ fill your wine rack with Château Margaux

☐ ☐ ☐ learn the difference between a crevice and a crevasse

☐ ☐ ☐ wear a zoot suit

☐ ☐ ☐ explore Angkor Wat in Angkor, Siem Reap, Cambodia

☐ ☐ ☐ reach wizard mode on a pinball game

☐ ☐ ☐ see the world's biggest cowboy boots in San Antonio, Texas

☐ ☐ ☐ look under a Scotsman's kilt

☐ ☐ ☐ get dirty at a Holi celebration

☐ ☐ ☐ go vegan

☐ ☐ ☐ learn to read lips

☐ ☐ ☐ drive an old Land Rover around an African
game reserve

☐ ☐ ☐ chug a soda and burp your name

☐ ☐ ☐ eat a cherimoya

☐ ☐ ☐ practise Pilates

☐ ☐ ☐ collect Le Creuset

☐ ☐ ☐ visit the Giant's
Causeway in Northern Ireland

☐ ☐ ☐ try IV vitamin therapy

☐ ☐ ☐ watch a tumbleweed tumble

☐ ☐ ☐ attend the Montreux Jazz Festival
in Switzerland

☐ ☐ ☐ recite the seven words you can't say on TV
according to George Carlin

☐ ☐ ☐ take the scenic route along Great Ocean
Road in Australia

☐ ☐ ☐ perform *seva* (also *sewa*)

☐ ☐ ☐ make paprika lattes a thing

☐ ☐ ☐ see a Broadway play

☐ ☐ ☐ see an Off-Broadway play

☐ ☐ ☐ see an Off-Off-Broadway play

☐ ☐ ☐ paint a mural

☐ ☐ ☐ visit the heart-shaped
Galešnjak Island in Croatia

☐ ☐ ☐ pour the perfect
champagne pyramid

☐ ☐ ☐ MacGyver your way out
of something

☐ ☐ ☐ jump out of a cake

☐ ☐ ☐ read all of David
Sedaris's books

☐ ☐ ☐ drink at the revolving
Carousel Piano Bar & Lounge at Hotel
Monteleone in New Orleans, Louisiana

bucket	f*ck it	done it	

☐☐☐ listen to krautrock

☐☐☐ ride the Orient Express

☐☐☐ adopt a rockabilly aesthetic

☐☐☐ do a standing front flip

☐☐☐ do a standing back flip

☐☐☐ visit Surprise Cave in Halong Bay, Vietnam

☐☐☐ amass crypto wealth

☐☐☐ eat *cuy* in Ecuador

☐☐☐ retaliate against someone who didn't provide a spoiler alert

☐☐☐ read yesterday's horoscope to see if it was true

HOROSCOPES
TAURUS --------
YOU WILL DIE TODAY

☐☐☐ walk the red carpet

☐☐☐ watch a building being demolished

☐☐☐ strip off for the World Naked Bike Ride

☐☐☐ live off the grid

☐ ☐ ☐ order the *omakase* service at a
sushi restaurant

☐ ☐ ☐ join the Saint Stupid's Day Parade in
San Francisco, California

☐ ☐ ☐ flambé your heart out and make
Bananas Foster

☐ ☐ ☐ ask someone for a 68 and promise to give
them 1 later

☐ ☐ ☐ go inside a lighthouse

☐ ☐ ☐ meet a Cree healer

☐ ☐ ☐ talk your way out of a speeding ticket

☐ ☐ ☐ hike through the Coloured Canyon in Egypt

☐ ☐ ☐ proudly call yourself a feminist

☐ ☐ ☐ get cosy in a Fair Isle sweater

☐ ☐ ☐ pee your name in the snow

☐ ☐ ☐ wow someone with the factoid that urine is
cleaner than spit

☐ ☐ ☐ wear a kaftan

☐ ☐ ☐ walk through the Ubud Monkey Forest in Bali, Indonesia

☐ ☐ ☐ ski indoors at the Mall of the Emirates in Dubai, United Arab Emirates

☐ ☐ ☐ organise a clothing swap

NEW HAGGIS FLAVOR!
POCKY

☐ ☐ ☐ swim in an infinity pool

☐ ☐ ☐ identify as a size queen

☐ ☐ ☐ taste every flavour of Pocky

☐ ☐ ☐ make ceviche

☐ ☐ ☐ check out a sneakerhead's collection

☐ ☐ ☐ practise Wicca

☐ ☐ ☐ grow a playoff beard

☐ ☐ ☐ gamble at the Venetian in Las Vegas, Nevada

☐ ☐ ☐ gamble at the Venetian in Macao, China

☐ ☐ ☐ talk someone out of socks and sandals

☐ ☐ ☐ meet a witch in Salem, Massachusetts

☐ ☐ ☐ drink kvass on the street in Kiev, Ukraine

☐ ☐ ☐ implement life hacks into your routine

☐ ☐ ☐ eat deep-fried pickles

☐ ☐ ☑ use whisky stones instead of ice cubes

☐ ☐ ☐ watch only sitcoms without laugh tracks

☐ ☐ ☐ shop at the Portobello Road Market in London

☐ ☐ ☐ taste the Spanish breast-shaped Tetilla cheese

☐ ☐ ☐ look at every single star on the Hollywood
Walk of Fame in California

☐ ☐ ☐ dress up like a Gibson Girl

☐ ☐ ☐ sleep in a tree house

☐ ☐ ☐ prove your haters wrong

☐ ☐ ☐ play Debussy's "Clair de Lune" on a
toy piano

☐ ☐ ☐ witness millions of crabs migrate on
Christmas Island, Australia

☐ ☐ ☐ touch your tongue to your nose

☐ ☐ ☐ understand a Zen koan

☐ ☐ ☐ see the world's skinniest house in Warsaw, Poland

☐ ☐ ☐ call 1-900-MIX-A-LOT and see if baby got back

☐ ☐ ☐ spend the day at an animal sanctuary

☐ ☐ ☐ study alchemy

☐ ☐ ☐ cruise the Amazon

☐ ☐ ☐ wear a Borat mankini in public

☐ ☐ ☐ enter a wet T-shirt contest

☐ ☐ ☐ donate your winnings to a breast cancer charity

☐ ☐ ☐ celebrate Walpurgis Night in Sweden

☐ ☐ ☐ make ambrosia salad

☐ ☐ ☐ fool someone with a trompe l'oeil

☐ ☐ ☐ burrow under a pile of warm laundry

☐ ☐ ☐ visit the town of Dildo, Canada

☐ ☐ ☐ drink aloe vera juice

☐ ☐ ☐ go snowshoeing

☐ ☐ ☐ soak in a Japanese *onsen*

☐ ☐ ☐ write a think piece for your local paper

☐ ☐ ☐ cheer marathon runners on at the midway point

☐ ☐ ☐ practise contact improv

☐ ☐ ☐ watch the mass ascension at the Albuquerque International Balloon Fiesta in New Mexico

☐ ☐ ☐ measure how much water can fit into a ten-gallon hat

☐ ☐ ☐ make an important life decision with a Magic 8 Ball

☐ ☐ ☐ ingest Pop Rocks and Coke

☐ ☐ ☐ ride in a hydrofoil

☐ ☐ ☐ help keep Portland weird

☐ ☐ ☐ eat frog porridge in Singapore

OH F*CK NO

☐ ☐ ☐ speak Igpay Atinlay

☐ ☐ ☐ sail safely through the Graveyard of the Atlantic

☐ ☐ ☐ live in a mid-century modern house

☐ ☐ ☐ look up at the walls of the Todra Gorge in Morocco

☐ ☐ ☐ meet someone whose favourite colour is puce

☐ ☐ ☐ find out if your *dosha* is *vatta*, *pitta*, or *kapha*

☐ ☐ ☐ get lei'd in Hawaii

☐ ☐ ☐ get laid in Hawaii

☐ ☐ ☐ refuse to delete your Myspace account

☐ ☐ ☐ go trout tickling

☐ ☐ ☐ sniff jasmine oil to cheer up

☐ ☐ ☐ comb a guinea pig's hair

☐ ☐ ☐ eat currywurst in Berlin, Germany

☐ ☐ ☐ grow a Fu Manchu moustache

☐ ☐ ☐ find a geocache

bucket
f*ck it
done it

- [ ] [ ] [x] make someone blush
- [ ] [ ] [ ] play *petanque* in Provence, France
- [ ] [ ] [ ] complete a firewalk
- [ ] [ ] [ ] enter a pond-skimming competition
- [ ] [ ] [ ] perfect your touchdown end zone dance
- [ ] [ ] [ ] dig yourself a pool on Hot Water Beach on Mercury Bay in New Zealand
- [ ] [ ] [ ] go to a Robert Mapplethorpe exhibit
- [ ] [ ] [ ] ululate
- [ ] [ ] [x] listen to an audiobook instead of music on a road trip
- [ ] [ ] [x] watch a solar eclipse
- [ ] [ ] [ ] watch a lunar eclipse
- [ ] [ ] [ ] create your own family crest
- [ ] [ ] [ ] clear up your bacne
- [ ] [ ] [ ] visit the Valley of Balls in Shetpe, Kazakhstan
- [ ] [ ] [ ] drink the CrossFit Kool-Aid

bucket
f*ck it
done it

☐ ☐ ☐ wear black lipstick

☐ ☐ ☐ learn to love natto

☐ ☐ ☐ learn to paint by
watching Bob Ross

☐ ☐ ☐ study Celtic
mythology

☐ ☐ ☐ support local businesses

☐ ☐ ☐ explore the heel of Italy's boot

☐ ☐ ☐ solve a quadratic equation

☐ ☐ ☐ discover your spirit animal

☐ ☐ ☐ understand the Korean concept of *han*

☐ ☐ ☑ pinkie-swear

☐ ☐ ☐ experience a meet-cute

☐ ☐ ☐ drink yerba mate instead of coffee

☐ ☐ ☐ watch colourful prayer flags dance in the
Himalayan wind

☐ ☐ ☐ visit a spice farm in Goa, India

☐ ☐ ☐ meet Canada's hot Santa

☐ ☐ ☐ take up geometric tourism and visit antipodal countries

☐ ☐ ☐ admire Googie architecture in Southern California

☐ ☐ ☐ cleanse your crystals under a full moon

☐ ☐ ☐ get a Brazilian wax

☐ ☐ ☐ use "stop, collaborate, and listen" as your wedding vows

☐ ☐ ☐ swim through a kelp forest

☐ ☐ ☐ chew betel nut (at your own risk)

☐ ☐ ☐ chop onions without crying

☐ ☐ ☐ go wadi bashing

☐ ☐ ☐ eat a Frito pie

☐ ☐ ☐ play an alpenhorn

☐ ☐ ☐ visit ABBA: The Museum in Stockholm, Sweden

☐ ☐ ☐ fanboy over the Star Wars sets in Tunisia

☐ ☐ ☐ embrace your FUPA

☐ ☐ ☐ ride the length of the Trans-Siberian Railway

☐ ☐ ☐ work for a company that thinks less about the big I's and more about the little you's

☐ ☐ ☐ yarn bomb

☐ ☐ ☐ throw a successful surprise party

☐ ☐ ☐ watch all of Studio Ghibli's movies

☐ ☐ ☐ rock a pair of Sally Jessy Raphael glasses

☐ ☐ ☐ admit that you like **Comic Sans**

☐ ☐ ☐ have an atelier

☐ ☐ ☐ experiment with ecstatic dance

bucket / f*ck it

☐ ☐ ☐ explore Gaudí's Park Güell in Barcelona, Spain

☐ ☐ ☐ train to be a divemaster

☐ ☐ ☐ visit Disneyland in California

☐ ☐ ☐ visit Walt Disney World in Florida

☐ ☐ ☐ visit Disneyland Paris in France

☐ ☐ ☐ visit Hong Kong Disneyland in China

☐ ☐ ☐ visit Tokyo Disneyland in Japan

☐ ☐ ☐ visit Shanghai Disneyland in China

☐ ☐ ☐ start a trend

☐ ☐ ☐ get seats on the Monster Bridge for NASCAR

☐ ☐ ☐ use family cloth instead of toilet paper

☐ ☐ ☐ hug a redwood tree

bucket
f*ck it
done it

☐ ☐ ☐ don an inflatable sumo suit and wrestle

☐ ☐ ☐ prove that knocking on wood works

☐ ☐ ☐ trek to Machu Picchu in Peru

☐ ☐ ☐ ban the use of the word "literally" in
your presence

☐ ☐ ☐ catch blue crabs in Chesapeake Bay,
Maryland

☐ ☐ ☐ write a screenplay

☐ ☐ ☐ avail yourself of a bad habit

☐ ☐ ☐ watch a squirting cucumber shoot its load

☐ ☐ ☐ see the wild monkeys in Gibraltar

☐ ☐ ☐ identify as a dandy

☐ ☐ ☐ hold a tarantula

☐ ☐ ☐ stay in an Earthship

☐ ☐ ☐ eat *barfi* in India

☐ ☐ ☐ keep a dream journal

☐ ☐ ☐ puff puff pass

bucket	f*ck it	done it	
☐	☐	☐	get dirty in the Sulphur Springs mud pools in Saint Lucia
☐	☐	☐	study sacred geometry
☐	☐	☐	fake an orgasm in Katz's Deli in New York, New York
☐	☐	☐	stand next to a sunflower that is taller than you
☐	☐	☐	walk through a graveyard at night
☐	☐	☐	go to a show at the Grand Ole Opry in Nashville, Tennessee
☐	☐	☐	spell dirty words in your alphabet soup
☐	☐	☐	watch a caber toss
☐	☐	☐	couch surf
☐	☐	☐	visit the black and white Cemetery of Morne-à-l'eau in Guadeloupe
☐	☐	☐	make a wish at 11:11
☐	☐	☐	meet an EGOT
☐	☐	☐	take fencing lessons

☐ ☐ ☐ hear the clicking language of the !Kung people in Namibia

☐ ☐ ☐ wear yellow underwear on New Year's Eve for luck in the coming year

☐ ☐ ☐ be mistaken for someone famous

☐ ☐ ☐ find your way out of a corn maze

☐ ☐ ☐ follow your favourite food truck on Twitter

☐ ☐ ☐ get tickets to the TED Talks

☐ ☐ ☐ design your own skateboard deck

☐ ☐ ☐ skate the Big O in Montreal, Canada

☐ ☐ ☐ cheer for anyone except Manchester United

☐ ☐ ☐ see Lake Titicaca in Peru and refrain from giggling at the name

☐ ☐ ☐ practise Bartitsu

☐ ☐ ☐ drink horchata

☐ ☐ ☐ merit a drum roll

☐ ☐ ☐ draw fashion inspiration
from Iris Apfel

☐ ☐ ☐ describe something
as Kierkegaardian

☐ ☐ ☐ people-watch from
the Spanish Steps in
Rome, Italy

☐ ☐ ☐ admire the Ottoman houses in Berat, Albania

☐ ☐ ☐ attend the Sundance Film Festival in Utah

☐ ☐ ☐ give your Fleshlight a name

☐ ☐ ☐ host a monthly poker night

☐ ☐ ☐ read the dictionary to ameliorate
your vocabulary

☐ ☐ ☐ hike to the *Into the Wild* bus in Alaska

☐ ☐ ☐ collect vintage concert T-shirts

☐ ☐ ☐ try ditch jumping in the Netherlands

☐ ☐ ☐ take your frustration out on bubble wrap

☐ ☐ ☐ eat Halloumi cheese in Cyprus

bucket
f*ck it
done it

☐ ☐ ☐ see a manatee in the wild

☐ ☐ ☐ play beach volleyball

☐ ☐ ☐ refuse to wear beige

☐ ☐ ☐ master a yo-yo trick

☐ ☐ ☐ finish an all-day jawbreaker

☐ ☐ ☐ summit Mount Kilimanjaro in Tanzania

☐ ☐ ☐ live in a loft

☐ ☐ ☐ use ladybirds instead of pesticides in
your garden

☐ ☐ ☐ see the *American Gothic* house in Eldon, Iowa

bucket	f*ck it	done it	
☐	☐	☐	strip off and join a No Trousers Tube Ride
☐	☐	☐	pose for a picture with The Big Banana in Coffs Harbour, Australia
☐	☐	☐	zip line in Costa Rica
☐	☐	☐	wear only conflict-free diamonds
☐	☐	☐	get acupuncture
☐	☐	☐	go to a wine tasting and swallow more than you spit
☐	☐	☐	hit someone with birch branches as they exit a Russian banya
☐	☐	☐	break the fourth wall with the audience intentionally
☐	☐	☐	ogle the Cerne Abbas hill figure in Dorset
☐	☐	☐	shape a bonsai tree
☐	☐	☐	drink Pimm's No. 1 Cup
☐	☐	☐	drink Pimm's No. 3 Cup
☐	☐	☐	drink Pimm's No. 6 Cup

□ □ □   visit all of the European microstates: Andorra, Liechtenstein, Malta, Monaco, San Marino, Gibraltar, and Vatican City

□ □ □   take flying lessons

□ □ □   create a *haft sin* display for Nowruz

□ □ □   witness the Monarch butterfly migration in Mexico

□ □ □   dance like Napoleon Dynamite

□ □ □   use nunchuks

□ □ □   start a dinner club

□ □ □   cure somebody's case of the Mondays

□ □ □   stay at Villa Trapp in Salzburg, Austria

□ □ □   stay at the Trapp Family Lodge in Stowe, Vermont

□ □ □   debunk an old wives' tale

□ □ □   debunk a hoax

□ □ □   debunk an urban legend

☐ ☐ ☐ watch an archaeological dig in process

☐ ☐ ☐ read every issue of Harvey Pekar's
American Splendor

☐ ☐ ☐ go for a drive with the top down (yours or
the car's)

☐ ☐ ☐ visit the Pena Palace in Sintra, Portugal

☐ ☐ ☐ speed date

☐ ☐ ☐ dress up as the Great Cornholio
for Halloween

☐ ☐ ☐ add edible flowers to your salad

☐ ☐ ☐ learn the Dewey decimal system

☐ ☐ ☐ get a family heirloom appraised on
Antiques Roadshow

☐ ☐ ☐ go to a Yayoi Kusama exhibit

☐ ☐ ☐ swim in Lake Chargoggagoggmanchaugg-agoggchau-bunagungamaugg in Webster, Massachusetts

☐ ☐ ☐ don a hat and go to a Kentucky Derby party

☐ ☐ ☐ chant at a *kirtan*

☐ ☐ ☐ watch Danish Dogme films

☐ ☐ ☐ practise Freestyle BMX tricks

☐ ☐ ☐ make your own kombucha

☐ ☐ ☐ prancercise

☐ ☐ ☐ listen to someone's heart through a stethoscope

☐ ☐ ☐ wear an ascot

☐ ☐ ☐ eat quahogs in Rhode Island

☐ ☐ ☐ join the Travelers' Century Club

☐ ☐ ☐ go to a concert at the Hollywood Bowl in Los Angeles, California

☐ ☐ ☐ find your G-spot

☐ ☐ ☐ find your P-spot

☐ ☐ ☐ use a treadmill desk

☐ ☐ ☐ drink a pilsner in Prague, Czech Republic

☐ ☐ ☐ train for a triathlon

☐ ☐ ☐ learn to speak Spanish

☐ ☐ ☐ shop at a floating market in Bangkok, Thailand

☐ ☐ ☐ eat a Bluth-style frozen banana

☐ ☐ ☐ create visual poetry

☐ ☐ ☐ get a septum piercing

☐ ☐ ☐ hike to the top of Le Morne Brabant in Mauritius

☐ ☐ ☐ circumnavigate an island in a kayak

☐ ☐ ☐ whale watch off the coast of British Colombia, Canada

☐ ☐ ☐ eat a deep-fried Mars bar

☐ ☐ ☐ join the goddess movement

☐ ☐ ☐ compete on a game show or reality show

☐ ☐ ☐ eat a bowl of mannish water in Jamaica
and see if it makes you horny

☐ ☐ ☐ pan for gold

☐ ☐ ☐ listen to Norwegian black metal music

☐ ☐ ☐ raise backyard chickens

☐ ☐ ☐ go for a schvitz

☐ ☐ ☐ gun it on the autobahn

☐ ☐ ☐ chew gum in Singapore

☐ ☐ ☐ catch fireflies

☐ ☐ ☐ try falconry

☐ ☐ ☐ start a conversation with
"This one time at band camp..."

☐ ☐ ☐ ask for forgiveness, not permission

☐ ☐ ☐ read the Upanishads

☐ ☐ ☐ spice a recipe with za'atar

☐ ☐ ☐ leave your mark on a car at Cadillac Ranch in Amarillo, Texas

☐ ☐ ☐ fancy yourself a weekend warrior

☐ ☐ ☐ play dominoes

☐ ☐ ☐ receive a Maori *hongi* greeting

☐ ☐ ☐ see a pink fairy armadillo in Argentina

☐ ☐ ☐ order an egg cream at an American diner

☐ ☐ ☐ watch Muhammad Ali's bout "Thrilla in Manila"

☐ ☐ ☐ admire the inside-out aesthetic of the Centre Pompidou in Paris, France

☐ ☐ ☐ feed a pond full of koi

☐ ☐ ☐ drink yak milk in Bhutan

☐ ☐ ☐ watch a meteor shower

☐ ☐ ☐ celebrate Festivus

☐ ☐ ☐ date a lumbersexual

☐ ☐ ☐ go to a Rugby Sevens game

☐ ☐ ☐ flash your backstage pass at security

☐ ☐ ☐ soak in the Băile Herculane hot springs in Romania

☐ ☐ ☐ play the cowbell and see how often people ask for more

☐ ☐ ☐ spend the day in a hammock

☐ ☐ ☐ invent a new sandwich

☐ ☐ ☐ draw fashion inspiration from the movie *Clueless*

☐ ☐ ☐ drive a Bugatti Chiron

☐ ☐ ☐ try AcroYoga

☐ ☐ ☐ swim in the Seven Sacred Pools in Maui, Hawaii

☐ ☐ ☐ give someone a love bite

☐ ☐ ☐ adopt a mod aesthetic

☐ ☐ ☐ score your holy grail item in a charity shop

☐ ☐ ☐ eat at a *restavracija, gostilna, okrepčevalnica, krčma, slaščičarna* and *kavarna* in Slovenia

☐ ☐ ☐ bake vinegar pie

☐ ☐ ☐ go camping every weekend through the summer

☐ ☐ ☐ admit you like emo music

☐ ☐ ☐ watch a hurling match in Ireland

☐ ☐ ☐ compare Texas and Kansas barbecue and pick a favourite

☐ ☐ ☐ drink tomato wine

☐ ☐ ☐ join the no poo movement and stop washing your hair

☐ ☐ ☐ pedal a boat through Houhai in Beijing, China

☐ ☐ ☐ go to a book reading

☐ ☐ ☐ throw seed bombs into a vacant lot

☐ ☐ ☐ wear an itsy-bitsy teeny-weeny yellow polka-dot bikini

☐ ☐ ☐ skeleton down a sled track

☐ ☐ ☐ see Mill Ends Park in Portland, Oregon – the world's smallest park

☐ ☐ ☐ eat escargot

☐ ☐ ☐ eat frogs' legs

☐ ☐ ☐ visit the desert oasis of Huacachina, Peru

☐ ☐ ☐ watch pimple-popping videos online
without puking

☐ ☐ ☐ meet friends in Chinatown for
dim sum

☐ ☐ ☐ bargain at a bazaar

☐ ☐ ☐ get a taste of expat life

☐ ☐ ☐ pose for a picture with Krampus instead
of Santa

☐ ☐ ☐ buy a pair of Louboutins

☐ ☐ ☐ study astrology

☐ ☐ ☐ study astronomy

☐ ☐ ☐ graduate from crossword puzzles to
cryptic crosswords

☐ ☐ ☐ admire the murals in the Lodhi Art District of
Delhi, India

☐ ☐ ☐ hire a decorator and take all the credit

☐ ☐ ☐ go to a Lucha Libre match in Mexico City, Mexico

☐ ☐ ☐ see a nuraghe megalith in Sardinia, Italy

☐ ☐ ☐ drink bubble tea

☐ ☐ ☐ enter a pie-eating contest

☐ ☐ ☐ polka

☐ ☐ ☐ walk through a bamboo forest

☐ ☐ ☐ identity as a boulevardier

☐ ☐ ☐ dress like David Bowie circa Ziggy Stardust

☐ ☐ ☐ swim in the Islands Brygge sea baths in Copenhagen, Denmark

☐ ☐ ☐ choose your stripper name even if you'll never be one

☐ ☐ ☐ listen to cowboy poetry

☐ ☐ ☐ watch cars navigate Lombard Street in San Francisco, California

☐ ☐ ☐ meet your teen idol

☐ ☐ ☐ compose a power ballad

☐ ☐ ☐ attend the Cannes Film Festival in France

☐ ☐ ☐ walk the length of West Highland Way
in Scotland

☐ ☐ ☐ rickroll someone

☐ ☐ ☐ go to a luau

☐ ☐ ☐ take up satellite watching

☐ ☐ ☐ scream like Edvard Munch's painting would
if it could

☐ ☐ ☐ play *tejo* in Colombia

☐ ☐ ☐ memorise all four versions of Adam Sandler's
"The Chanukah Song"

☐ ☐ ☐ try EFT

☐ ☐ ☐ draw a self-portrait

☐ ☐ ☐ ignore anyone who refers to themselves as a
"human being rather than a human doing"

☐ ☐ ☐ leave a bottle of Jack Daniel's on
Lemmy's grave

☐ ☐ ☐ ride a penny-farthing

☐ ☐ ☐ play the sitar

☐ ☐ ☐ see a giant squid

☐ ☐ ☐ take the Interislander ferry between North
Island and South Island in New Zealand

☐ ☐ ☐ freedive

☐ ☐ ☐ stay at the Fairmont Château Lake Louise in
Alberta, Canada

☐ ☐ ☐ burn copal instead of incense

☐ ☐ ☐ eat key lime pie in the Florida Keys

☐ ☐ ☐ pet a hairless cat
à la Dr Evil

☐ ☐ ☐ find your *ikigai*

☐ ☐ ☐ propagate your succulents

☐ ☐ ☐ put hotels on Mayfair right before someone
lands on it

☐ ☐ ☐ go on a wine tour in Stellenbosch,
South Africa

☐ ☐ ☐ buy an Arne Jacobsen Egg chair

☐ ☐ ☐ have a dolphin-assisted birth

☐ ☐ ☐ complete Dry January

☐ ☐ ☐ win a game of conkers

☐ ☐ ☐ search for Wroclaw's dwarfs in Poland

☐ ☐ ☐ stop waiting for the other shoe to drop

☐ ☐ ☐ see a blood moon

☐ ☐ ☐ join a flash mob

☐ ☐ ☐ make only retro 1950s
recipes for a week

ASPIC
100 WAYS
—VOL I—

BY GELATINA MOULDÉ

☐ ☐ ☐ stick your gum on
Bubblegum Alley in
San Luis Obispo, California

☐ ☐ ☐ stick your gum on the Market Theater
Gum Wall in Seattle, Washington

☐ ☐ ☐ affix a hex sign to your house

☐ ☐ ☐ spot the big five while on safari

☐ ☐ ☐ play chess in Washington Square Park in New York, New York

☐ ☐ ☐ crochet granny squares

☐ ☐ ☐ refer to weed as the devil's lettuce

☐ ☐ ☐ practise Vipassana meditation

☐ ☐ ☐ dip your toes in the Labrador Sea

☐ ☐ ☐ clog dance

☐ ☐ ☐ eat fairy bread

☐ ☐ ☐ eat *hagelslag*

☐ ☐ ☐ dress like Sharon Stone circa *Casino*

☐ ☐ ☐ drink Moxie in Maine

☐ ☐ ☐ master the one-handed egg crack

☐ ☐ ☐ go to an Ai Weiwei exhibit

☐ ☐ ☐ fish in Caribou Penis Lake in Quebec, Canada

☐ ☐ ☐ watch all of Fellini's movies

☐ ☐ ☐ learn to say "thank you" in five different languages

bucket	f*ck it	done it	
☐	☐	☐	enrol at the Sorbonne
☐	☐	☐	go to a foam party
☐	☐	☐	buy a stack of books at Powell's City of Books in Portland, Oregon
☐	☐	☐	buy a stack of books at the Strand Book Store in New York, New York
☐	☐	☐	buy a stack of books at Pulpfiction Books in Vancouver, Canada
☐	☐	☐	buy a stack of books at Shakespeare and Company in Paris, France
☐	☐	☐	identify as a Ravenclaw
☐	☐	☐	identify as a Hufflepuff
☐	☐	☐	identify as a Slytherin
☐	☐	☐	identify as a Gryffindor
☐	☐	☐	use Occam's razor to solve a problem
☐	☐	☐	overcome your fear of public speaking
☐	☐	☐	admire the Timurid architecture in Uzbekistan

bucket
f*ck it
done it

☐ ☐ ☐ "live every week like it's Shark Week"

☐ ☐ ☐ do a crossword in pen

☐ ☐ ☐ create an ambigram

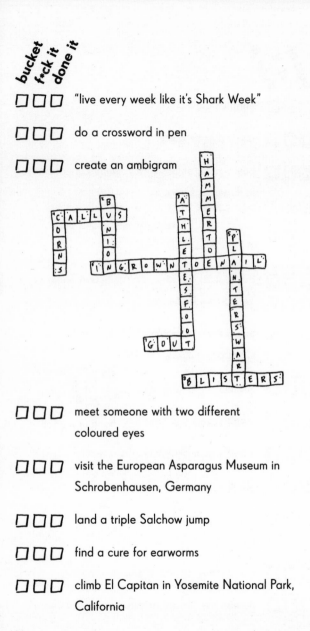

☐ ☐ ☐ meet someone with two different
coloured eyes

☐ ☐ ☐ visit the European Asparagus Museum in
Schrobenhausen, Germany

☐ ☐ ☐ land a triple Salchow jump

☐ ☐ ☐ find a cure for earworms

☐ ☐ ☐ climb El Capitan in Yosemite National Park,
California

☐ ☐ ☐ find a chaga mushroom in the forest

☐ ☐ ☐ eat fried courgette blossoms

☐ ☐ ☐ collect Hello Kitty memorabilia

☐ ☐ ☐ see a jingle truck in Pakistan

☐ ☐ ☐ pick pawpaws in West Virginia

☐ ☐ ☐ identify as an activist

☐ ☐ ☐ make a reservation under the name
Ben Dover

☐ ☐ ☐ use a voodoo doll

☐ ☐ ☐ take part in *hanami* in Japan in the spring

☐ ☐ ☐ take part in *momijigari* in Japan in the fall

☐ ☐ ☐ brush your teeth with charcoal toothpaste

☐ ☐ ☐ go kitesurfing

☐ ☐ ☐ get a face tattoo

☐ ☐ ☐ recreate Mr Whippy at home

☐ ☐ ☐ celebrate Something on a Stick Day

bucket
f*ck it
done it

☐ ☐ ☐ see the *Seven Magic Mountains* art installation in Las Vegas, Nevada

☐ ☐ ☐ achieve a four-hour workweek

☐ ☐ ☐ listen to prog rock

☐ ☐ ☐ walk across the Millennium Bridge in London

☐ ☐ ☐ learn to love *surströmming*

☐ ☐ ☐ pray to Saint Fiacre to cure your hemorrhoids

☐ ☐ ☐ root for the underdog

☐ ☐ ☐ joust

☐ ☐ ☐ bury someone up to their neck in sand

☐ ☐ ☐ be buried up to your neck in sand

☐ ☐ ☐ ogle the *David* statue in Florence, Italy

☐ ☐ ☐ go to all of the Cirque du Soleil shows

☐ ☐ ☐ volunteer at a charity car wash

☐ ☐ ☐ have a kilt made with your family tartan

☐ ☐ ☐ watch Nathan's Hot Dog Eating Contest in Coney Island, New York

☐ ☐ ☐ drink mint tea in Morocco

☐ ☐ ☐ replace your dining room table with table football

☐ ☐ ☐ practise your "O Face" before a hot date

☐ ☐ ☐ play a Gibson Flying V guitar

☐ ☐ ☐ eat conch chowder

☐ ☐ ☐ stop cracking your knuckles

☐ ☐ ☐ elope

☐ ☐ ☐ dress up as a priest and go to Ted Fest in Ireland

☐ ☐ ☐ bid at an auction

☐ ☐ ☐ crack a wheel of Parmigiano-Reggiano cheese

☐ ☐ ☐ surf in Teahupo'o, Tahiti

☐ ☐ ☐ go back-to-school shopping, even if you aren't
a student

☐ ☐ ☐ learn sign language

☐ ☐ ☐ take a Thai cooking class

☐ ☐ ☐ see the Banaue rice terraces in the Philippines

☐ ☐ ☐ drive by the Eames House in Pacific
Palisades, California

☐ ☐ ☐ skip the skiing and focus on the après-ski

☐ ☐ ☐ fool a carnivore with seitan

☐ ☐ ☐ keep a bottle of vodka in your freezer at
all times

☐ ☐ ☐ slide down the banister at the Hotel
Palacio del Retiro in Madrid, Spain

☐ ☐ ☐ start a blog

☐ ☐ ☐ make latkes

☐ ☐ ☐ refuse to give credence to the Manic Pixie
Dream Girl

☐ ☐ ☐ try logrolling

- ☐ ☐ ☐ record a demo at a studio
- ☐ ☐ ☐ get a weekly mani/pedi
- ☐ ☐ ☐ go on a moose safari in Norway
- ☐ ☐ ☐ shave your entire body
- ☐ ☐ ☐ drink a Blue Hawaiian in Hawaii
- ☐ ☐ ☐ see Niagara Falls in Canada/United States
- ☐ ☐ ☐ see Iguazu Falls in Brazil/Argentina
- ☐ ☐ ☐ see Victoria Falls in Zimbabwe/Zambia
- ☐ ☐ ☐ see Angel Falls in Venezuela
- ☐ ☐ ☐ twerk
- ☐ ☐ ☐ witness a faith healing
- ☐ ☐ ☐ enter the Air Guitar Championships in Finland
- ☐ ☐ ☐ observe an expert tracker in action
- ☐ ☐ ☐ join a bowling league
- ☐ ☐ ☐ spend a Sunday antiquing

☐ ☐ ☐ watch a game of Basque pelota

☐ ☐ ☐ attend the DEF CON hacking conference in
Las Vegas, Nevada

☐ ☐ ☐ train to be a sommelier

☐ ☐ ☐ go bouldering

☐ ☐ ☐ look up at the lanterns in Hoi An, Vietnam

☐ ☐ ☐ peg your jeans

☐ ☐ ☐ peg your boyfriend

☐ ☐ ☐ stay at a boutique hotel

☐ ☐ ☐ eat curried goat in the Caribbean

☐ ☐ ☐ paddle an outrigger canoe

☐ ☐ ☐ undergo hypnosis

☐ ☐ ☐ visit the Bay of Fires in Tasmania, Australia

☐ ☐ ☐ write your acceptance speech before
being nominated

☐ ☐ ☐ build a giant house of cards

☐ ☐ ☐ listen to all of the MTV Unplugged albums

bucket	f*ck it	done it	

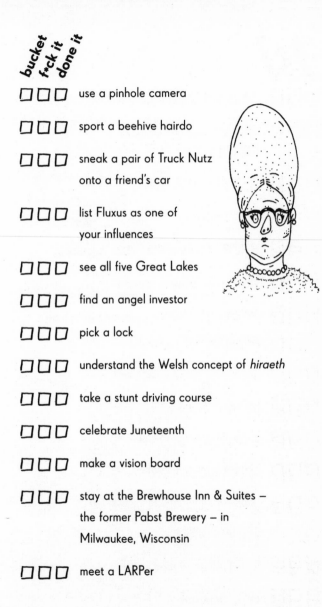

☐ ☐ ☐ use a pinhole camera

☐ ☐ ☐ sport a beehive hairdo

☐ ☐ ☐ sneak a pair of Truck Nutz onto a friend's car

☐ ☐ ☐ list Fluxus as one of your influences

☐ ☐ ☐ see all five Great Lakes

☐ ☐ ☐ find an angel investor

☐ ☐ ☐ pick a lock

☐ ☐ ☐ understand the Welsh concept of *hiraeth*

☐ ☐ ☐ take a stunt driving course

☐ ☐ ☐ celebrate Juneteenth

☐ ☐ ☐ make a vision board

☐ ☐ ☐ stay at the Brewhouse Inn & Suites – the former Pabst Brewery – in Milwaukee, Wisconsin

☐ ☐ ☐ meet a LARPer

☐ ☐ ☐ complete a pommel horse routine

☐ ☐ ☐ see the Wassu stone circles
in Gambia

☐ ☐ ☐ organise a street party

☐ ☐ ☐ study Dadaism

☐ ☐ ☐ drive the length of Ruta 40 in Argentina

☐ ☐ ☐ wear velvet smoking slippers

☐ ☐ ☐ describe an art piece as derivative to hide
your ignorance

☐ ☐ ☐ get a hole in one at mini golf

☐ ☐ ☐ visit all of Frank Gehry's buildings

☐ ☐ ☐ score the game-winning point

☐ ☐ ☐ choose a go-to karaoke song

☐ ☐ ☐ drink kölsch in Cologne, Germany

☐ ☐ ☐ pop your collar

☐ ☐ ☐ watch a horned toad squirt blood from its eyes

☐ ☐ ☐ travel by private jet

bucket
f*ck it
done it

☐ ☐ ☐ refer to the early 2000s as the aughts

☐ ☐ ☐ go to the top of the Gateway Arch in Saint Louis, Missouri

☐ ☐ ☐ describe something as scrumdiddlyumptious

☐ ☐ ☐ install a rain barrel in your garden

☐ ☐ ☐ drink *mamajuana* in the Dominican Republic and see if it makes you horny

☐ ☐ ☐ revel in your delusions of grandeur

☐ ☐ ☐ improve the feng shui in your home

☐ ☐ ☐ part your hair on the opposite side

☐ ☐ ☐ speak Klingon

☐ ☐ ☐ practise kendo

☐ ☐ ☐ write down every compliment you receive

☐ ☐ ☐ reread them when you feel like crap

☐ ☐ ☐ throw a coin in the Trevi Fountain to ensure your return to Rome, Italy

bucket
f*ck it
done it

☐ ☐ ☐ stay in an Airstream trailer

☐ ☐ ☐ "elevate small talk to medium talk"

☐ ☐ ☐ use argan oil on your skin

☐ ☐ ☐ see an argan tree full of goats in Morocco

☐ ☐ ☐ feel a pregnant belly as the baby is kicking

☐ ☐ ☐ make Guy Fieri's Mac-Daddi-Roni Salad

☐ ☐ ☐ sit courtside for an NBA game

☐ ☐ ☐ hike the length of the Dragon's Back in
Hong Kong, China

☐ ☐ ☐ follow the Stanislavsky method of acting

☐ ☐ ☐ pour the perfect pint of Guinness

☐ ☐ ☐ acquire the internet domain of your name

☐ ☐ ☐ shop at the Witches' Market in La Paz, Bolivia

☐ ☐ ☐ tell someone if they have something green in
their teeth

☐ ☐ ☐ witness a Candomblé ritual

☐ ☐ ☐ vajazzle your vajayjay

☐ ☐ ☐ walk up Canton Avenue in Pittsburgh, Pennsylvania – the steepest street in the United States

☐ ☐ ☐ watch all of Spike Lee's movies

☐ ☐ ☐ build a cobhouse

☐ ☐ ☐ drink EntoMilk

☐ ☐ ☐ eat pierogis in Poland

☐ ☐ ☐ gallop down a beach on horseback

☐ ☐ ☐ burn anything that says "Keep Calm and Carry On"

☐ ☐ ☐ support your local queens and go to a drag show

☐ ☐ ☐ date a silver fox

☐ ☐ ☐ expose a charlatan

☐ ☐ ☐ turn your living room into a shrine to Danish design

☐ ☐ ☐ infiltrate the Skull and Bones at Yale

bucket	f*ck it	done it	
☐	☐	☐	go car park pimping in Botswana
☐	☐	☐	try axe throwing
☐	☐	☐	ring a bell in a tower
☐	☐	☐	complete a juice cleanse
☐	☐	☐	host an Ugly Christmas Sweater Party
☐	☐	☐	drink ice wine in Niagara-on-the-Lake, Canada
☐	☐	☐	do a comedy set on amateur night
☐	☐	☐	speak Yiddish
☐	☐	☐	go spearfishing
☐	☐	☐	break-dance
☐	☐	☐	take the scenic route along the Grande Corniche in the South of France
☐	☐	☐	give a mansplainer a slow clap
☐	☐	☐	endow a scholarship at your alma mater
☐	☐	☐	ride in a Baja Bug
☐	☐	☐	tour the Neon Museum in Las Vegas, Nevada

☐ ☐ ☐ tell someone they've taken to something "like a cow to cud"

☐ ☐ ☐ climb the Seven Summits

☐ ☐ ☐ cut off someone's man bun (with their permission)

☐ ☐ ☐ taste Perique tobacco liqueur

☐ ☐ ☐ keep a houseplant alive that isn't a cactus

☐ ☐ ☐ sit on the Princess Diana bench at the Taj Mahal in India

☐ ☐ ☐ ride fakie on your snowboard

☐ ☐ ☐ eat squid jerky

☐ ☐ ☐ gaze into a crystal ball and try scrying

☐ ☐ ☐ visit the city of Unalaska in Alaska

☐ ☐ ☐ lasso

☐ ☐ ☐ test all of the functions on a Japanese toilet

☐ ☐ ☐ navigate a Scandinavian fjord

☐ ☐ ☐ navigate a Mediterranean calanque

☐ ☐ ☐ navigate a Scottish firth

☐ ☐ ☐ navigate an Omani khor

☐ ☐ ☐ grow muttonchop whiskers

☐ ☐ ☐ kiss someone after getting your mouth frozen
at the dentist

☐ ☐ ☐ pick a peck of pickled peppers

☐ ☐ ☐ learn to eat fire

☐ ☐ ☐ see a lemur in the wilds of Madagascar

☐ ☐ ☐ drive by the house you grew up in to see if
it's changed

☐ ☐ ☐ pan-fry some livermush and call it breakfast

☐ ☐ ☐ travel by jeepney in the Philippines

bucket	f*ck it	done it	
☐	☐	☐	use a scythe
☐	☐	☐	write with a quill
☐	☐	☐	spot a Fata Morgana on the horizon
☐	☐	☐	bang a gavel
☐	☐	☐	embrace your resting bitch face
☐	☐	☐	fearlessly bite into a balut in the Philippines
☐	☐	☐	create an altar in your home
☐	☐	☐	walk across the Brooklyn Bridge in New York, New York
☐	☐	☐	buy a whole canned chicken
☐	☐	☐	go to an eSports tournament
☐	☐	☐	admire an Os Gemeos mural
☐	☐	☐	find someone who loves you like Oprah loves Gayle
☐	☐	☐	champion for more wheelchair accessibility
☐	☐	☐	participate in a mock duel
☐	☐	☐	spice a recipe with harissa

☐ ☐ ☐ drink moose milk in Bjurholm, Sweden

☐ ☐ ☐ join a pub quiz team

☐ ☐ ☐ crank a Victrola

☐ ☐ ☐ Netflix and chill with a cute neighbour

☐ ☐ ☐ win the biggest stuffed
animal at the fair

☐ ☐ ☐ take the Rorschach
inkblot test

☐ ☐ ☐ try finger-tutting

☐ ☐ ☐ make whoopie pies

☐ ☐ ☐ go on a wine tour in
Mendoza, Argentina

☐ ☐ ☐ experience a runner's high

☐ ☐ ☐ perform a Full Nelson

☐ ☐ ☐ perform a Half Nelson

☐ ☐ ☐ ask yourself, "What would Brian Boitano do?"

☐ ☐ ☐ visit Tivoli Gardens in Copenhagen, Denmark

☐ ☐ ☐ win a 50/50 draw

☐ ☐ ☐ climb the Sydney Harbour Bridge in Australia

☐ ☐ ☐ experience past life regression

☐ ☐ ☐ see Uranus through a telescope

☐ ☐ ☐ start your own Ultimate Frisbee league

☐ ☐ ☐ take a public stance on pineapple pizza

☐ ☐ ☐ stroll along the River Walk in
San Antonio, Texas

☐ ☐ ☐ play tennis on a grass court

☐ ☐ ☐ drink at an ice bar

☐ ☐ ☐ peel the stick figure family stickers off the back
of someone's minivan

☐ ☐ ☐ eat a *chivito* sandwich
in Uruguay

☐ ☐ ☐ take an archery
lesson

☐ ☐ ☐ pull ahead of the Peloton

bucket	f*ck it	done it	
☐	☐	☐	come up with a family motto
☐	☐	☐	drive by the Grey Gardens house in East Hampton, New York
☐	☐	☐	watch Eurovision
☐	☐	☐	buy sriracha by the case
☐	☐	☐	attend the Toronto International Film Festival in Canada
☐	☐	☐	retake SATs as an adult and see how you do
☐	☐	☐	fantasise that you're dating feminist Ryan Gosling
☐	☐	☐	go tubing down a lazy river
☐	☐	☐	make green eggs and ham for breakfast
☐	☐	☐	train to be a doula
☐	☐	☐	contribute to a crowdfunding campaign
☐	☐	☐	sandboard down Cerro Negro volcano in Nicaragua
☐	☐	☐	pilgrimage to White Castle

bucket
f*ck it
done it

☐ ☐ ☐ compete in the Escape from Alcatraz Triathlon in San Francisco, California

☐ ☐ ☐ cheer for anyone except Man United

☐ ☐ ☐ work as a WWOOFer (willing worker on organic farms)

☐ ☐ ☐ go on a polar bear tour in Churchill, Canada

☐ ☐ ☐ get cosy in an Aran sweater

☐ ☐ ☐ drink a rum swizzle in Bermuda

☐ ☐ ☐ buy only cruelty-free beauty products

☐ ☐ ☐ scour flea markets for undiscovered treasures

☐ ☐ ☐ ride the Great Scenic Railway at Luna Park in Melbourne, Australia

☐ ☐ ☐ play hacky sack

☐ ☐ ☐ quote Rumi

☐ ☐ ☐ refuse to shop on Black Friday

☐ ☐ ☐ party on Fire Island in New York

bucket
f*ck it
done it

☐☐☐ Google yourself and like what you see

☐☐☐ sip tea with your pinky sticking out

☐☐☐ meet someone with a third nipple

☐☐☐ ride in a rickshaw

☐☐☐ celebrate the vernal equinox

☐☐☐ celebrate the autumnal equinox

☐☐☐ visit a *ksar* in Tunisia

☐☐☐ embrace your dad bod

☐☐☐ master the knuckle hop

☐☐☐ strap on some crampons and go ice climbing

☐☐☐ embrace a *wabi-sabi* outlook

☐☐☐ see the *Thelma & Louise* cliff near Moab, Utah

☐☐☐ take your frustrations out at a batting cage

☐☐☐ sext

☐☐☐ watch a *bokator* match in Cambodia

☐ ☐ ☐   read all of *Grimms' Fairy Tales*

☐ ☐ ☐   learn how to tell if a pineapple is ripe

☐ ☐ ☐   ride a hoverboard

☐ ☐ ☐   drink Mexican hot chocolate

☐ ☐ ☐   protect your lucky fishing lure at all costs

☐ ☐ ☐   get a suit made on Savile Row

☐ ☐ ☐   swim in a lagoon in New Caledonia

☐ ☐ ☐   find out what Meatloaf meant by "but I won't do that"

☐ ☐ ☐   become an eBay PowerSeller

☐ ☐ ☐   visit Georgia O'Keeffe's house in Abiquiú, New Mexico

☐ ☐ ☐   tailgate

☐ ☐ ☐   do the worm on the dance floor of an exclusive club

☐ ☐ ☐   make your own hemp milk

☐ ☐ ☐   tell someone they have chutzpah

☐ ☐ ☐ see a blue-footed booby in the wild

☐ ☐ ☐ take the Jadrolinija Ferry from Split to Hvar in Croatia

☐ ☐ ☐ hang out in a Western-style saloon

☐ ☐ ☐ get your ears candled

☐ ☐ ☐ smoke a hookah

☐ ☐ ☐ give up your vices

☐ ☐ ☐ audition for the Blue Man Group

☐ ☐ ☐ toilet train your cat

☐ ☐ ☐ ride the Ferris wheel at Luna Park in Beirut, Lebanon

☐ ☐ ☐ watch a concert from the wings of the stage

☐ ☐ ☐ do your Kegels religiously

☐ ☐ ☐ speak Polari

☐ ☐ ☐ eat a Hot Brown in Louisville, Kentucky

☐ ☐ ☐ enter a watercross competition

☐ ☐ ☐ carve a white pumpkin for Halloween

☐ ☐ ☐ tie a cherry stem into a knot with your tongue

☐ ☐ ☐ take a siesta in Spain

☐ ☐ ☐ take a *riposo* in Italy

☐ ☐ ☐ moonlight in your dream career

☐ ☐ ☐ quit your day job

☐ ☐ ☐ admit that you're too lazy for foreplay

☐ ☐ ☐ make a citizen's arrest

☐ ☐ ☐ ice-skate in Gorky Park in
Moscow, Russia

☐ ☐ ☐ embrace freeganism

☐ ☐ ☐ go for afternoon tea
with your mum

☐ ☐ ☐ listen to *The White Album* by the Beatles

☐ ☐ ☐ listen to *The Black Album* by Jay-Z

☐ ☐ ☐ complete an obstacle race

☐ ☐ ☐ cruise the Mekong

☐ ☐ ☐ French exit a party

☐ ☐ ☐ buy a *nakshi kantha* quilt from Bangladesh

☐ ☐ ☐ watch a film noir marathon

☐ ☐ ☐ go all fashion police on someone's ass

☐ ☐ ☐ leave a fez on Tommy Cooper's grave

☐ ☐ ☐ visit the *Prada Marfa* in Texas

☐ ☐ ☐ ride a Segway

☐ ☐ ☐ navigate the roundabout around L'Arc de Triomphe in Paris, France

☐ ☐ ☐ get up early and watch the sunrise

☐ ☐ ☐ learn the Latin names for all your plants

THEY SEE ME ROLLIN'

☐ ☐ ☐ be impervious to clickbait

☐ ☐ ☐ watch a goat race in Tobago

☐ ☐ ☐ attend the Adult Space Academy in Alabama

☐ ☐ ☐ make a long-distance relationship work

☐ ☐ ☐ tattoo "sun's out, guns out" on your bicep

☐ ☐ ☐ drink Screech in Newfoundland, Canada

☐ ☐ ☐ star in a one-person show

☐ ☐ ☐ eat a kolacky

☐ ☐ ☐ play backgammon

☐ ☐ ☐ flip a pancake like a boss

☐ ☐ ☐ walk along the canals of Venice, California

☐ ☐ ☐ walk along the canals of Venice, Italy

☐ ☐ ☐ collect beer steins

☐ ☐ ☐ ride in a vintage car in Havana, Cuba

☐ ☐ ☐ join the International Guild of Knot Tyers

☐ ☐ ☐ get a tongue piercing

☐ ☐ ☐ drink bulletproof coffee (if you must)

☐ ☐ ☐ place a *maneki-neko* near your front door
for luck

☐ ☐ ☐ downsize and move into a tiny house

☐ ☐ ☐ take up gnoming

☐ ☐ ☐ fly over the Nazca Lines in Peru.

☐ ☐ ☐ put an amethyst in your drink and see if you still get drunk

☐ ☐ ☐ organise a body positive photo shoot

☐ ☐ ☐ wear a beret

☐ ☐ ☐ visit the Acropolis in Athens, Greece

☐ ☐ ☐ go cliff jumping

☐ ☐ ☐ watch *Mommie Dearest* on Mother's Day

☐ ☐ ☐ admit that you like country music

☐ ☐ ☐ order cherry pie at Twede's Cafe in North Bend, Washington

☐ ☐ ☐ perfect your roundhouse kick

☐ ☐ ☐ make pruno

☐ ☐ ☐ enter a competitive hobbyhorse championship

☐ ☐ ☐ tour Potala Palace in Lhasa, Tibet

☐ ☐ ☐ sleep in an igloo

☐ ☐ ☐ build a smokehouse in your back garden

☐ ☐ ☐ keep your narcissism
under control

☐ ☐ ☐ try road bowling in Ireland

☐ ☐ ☐ memorise a dirty limerick

☐ ☐ ☐ visit a Nordic stave church

☐ ☐ ☐ recreate Björk's swan dress
and wear it to prom

☐ ☐ ☐ do the Bend and Snap near your
crush and see what happens

☐ ☐ ☐ ride a camel

☐ ☐ ☐ practise paganism

☐ ☐ ☐ eat poutine in Canada

☐ ☐ ☐ keep a jar of *giardiniera* in your fridge at all times

☐ ☐ ☐ refer to the internet as the information superhighway

☐ ☐ ☐ sell out happily

☐ ☐ ☐ date a gamine

☐ ☐ ☐ squeeze in an afternoon delight on your lunch break

☐ ☐ ☐ move to a Blue Zone

☐ ☐ ☐ abide by PLUR

☐ ☐ ☐ watch *Die Hard* every Christmas

☐ ☐ ☐ visit a panda sanctuary in China

☐ ☐ ☐ drive an electric car

☐ ☐ ☐ go to a clambake

☐ ☐ ☐ resurrect your double Dutch skills

☐ ☐ ☐ build a blanket fort and sleep in it for a week

☐ ☐ ☐ hear a muezzin call to prayer

☐ ☐ ☐ drink apple cider in New England

☐ ☐ ☐ visit a cider house in San Sebastián, Spain

☐ ☐ ☐ juggle

☐ ☐ ☐ identify as a power bottom

☐ ☐ ☐ fill a humidor with all your favourite cigars

☐ ☐ ☐ have your tarot cards read

☐ ☐ ☐ run a half marathon

☐ ☐ ☐ run a marathon

☐ ☐ ☐ read a newspaper from
the day of your birth

DAILY NEWS
STRANGE BABY
BORN TODAY

☐ ☐ ☐ see your nemesis get
their comeuppance

☐ ☐ ☐ go TV-free for a year (even streaming)

☐ ☐ ☐ ogle the Bondi Beach lifeguards in
Sydney, Australia

☐ ☐ ☐ ride shotgun in the Oscar Mayer Wienermobile

☐ ☐ ☐ snap a whip

☐ ☐ ☐ plumb the depths of your psyche

☐ ☐ ☐ convince someone a headline from *The Onion* is real

☐ ☐ ☐ take a barre class

☐ ☐ ☐ shop at Shanghai Tang in Hong Kong, China

☐ ☐ ☐ get scrubbed down at a hammam

☐ ☐ ☐ trust your gut instead of a guru

☐ ☐ ☐ feed someone grapes one by one

☐ ☐ ☐ tour the Rock and Roll Hall of Fame in Cleveland, Ohio

☐ ☐ ☐ understand the Swedish concept of *lagom*

☐ ☐ ☐ eat goulash

☐ ☐ ☐ see someone's aura

☐ ☐ ☐ watch all of Bruce Lee's movies

☐ ☐ ☐ tour the Waitomo Glowworm Caves in New Zealand

☐ ☐ ☐ wear a talisman

☐ ☐ ☐ ride the SLUT (South Lake Union Trolley) in Seattle, Washington

☐ ☐ ☐ attend an art battle

☐ ☐ ☐ witness an event that dramatically changes history

☐ ☐ ☐ adopt a macrobiotic diet

☐ ☐ ☐ "put a bird on it"

☐ ☐ ☐ make Indian pickle

☐ ☐ ☐ join an Ultimate Frisbee team

☐ ☐ ☐ go to an Amy Schumer show and be thankful HPV isn't airborne

☐ ☐ ☐ drink Brennivín in Iceland

☐ ☐ ☐ watch a snake charmer in action

☐ ☐ ☐ nap every day for a year

☐ ☐ ☐ pose for boudoir photos

☐☐☐ donate blood

☐☐☐ try hog calling

☐☐☐ donate breast milk

☐☐☐ buy box seats for a game

☐☐☐ get dirty during the flour fight on
Clean Monday in Galaxidi, Greece

☐☐☐ skimboard

☐☐☐ wear a muff instead
of gloves

☐☐☐ read Hafez's ghazels

☐☐☐ sport a Bettie
Page hairdo

☐☐☐ tango

☐☐☐ adopt a pet hedgehog

☐☐☐ spot a spirit bear in the wilds of British
Columbia, Canada

☐☐☐ sail safely through the Graveyard of
the Pacific

bucket	f*ck it	done it	

☐ ☐ ☐ witness an avalanche from a safe distance

☐ ☐ ☐ visit the town of Twatt in Scotland

☐ ☐ ☐ create a cabinet of curiosities

☐ ☐ ☐ dress like Jack White circa *Elephant*

☐ ☐ ☐ sleep in a haunted house

☐ ☐ ☐ drive an amphibious vehicle into the water

☐ ☐ ☐ enter the World Wife-Carrying Championship in Finland

☐ ☐ ☐ champion for a husband-carrying competition

☐ ☐ ☐ explore Niki de Saint Phalle's Tarot Garden in Tuscany, Italy

☐ ☐ ☐ taste Cynar artichoke liqueur

☐ ☐ ☐ ghost someone who deserves it

☐ ☐ ☐ uncover your fortune with a metal detector on a stretch of sand

☐ ☐ ☐ nail a muscle-up

☐ ☐ ☐ give each of the deadly sins a try

☐ ☐ ☐ see a bloat of hippopotami

☐ ☐ ☐ summit Mount Fuji

☐ ☐ ☐ get *yakin* burned into your walking stick at
each station on the way up Mount Fuji

☐ ☐ ☐ find out your moon sign

☐ ☐ ☐ spend your rent money at Amoeba Music in
Hollywood, California

☐ ☐ ☐ give your partner your "Freebie List"

☐ ☐ ☐ try cooking sous vide instead of barbecuing

☐ ☐ ☐ drink caipirinhas in Brazil

☐ ☐ ☐ attend the ESPY Awards

☐ ☐ ☐ assert yourself as the alpha in your dog's life

☐ ☐ ☐ attend a family reunion with
four generations represented

☐ ☐ ☐ avoid anyone who says they have
the gift of the gab

☐ ☐ ☐ refuse to be a monoglot

bucket	f*ck it	done it	
☐	☐	☐	become bilingual
☐	☐	☐	wear a fascinator
☐	☐	☐	try fartlek training
☐	☐	☐	gather your cojones and eat stink heads in Alaska
☐	☐	☐	have your home featured on Design*Sponge
☐	☐	☐	attend the National Arts Festival in Grahamstown, South Africa
☐	☐	☐	find a cure for "baby brain"
☐	☐	☐	pop a wheelie
☐	☐	☐	soak in the Dunton Hot Springs in Dolores, Colorado
☐	☐	☐	go to a Stephen Sondheim musical
☐	☐	☐	eat at a Michelin-starred restaurant
☐	☐	☐	tiptoe through the tulips at Keukenhof in the Netherlands
☐	☐	☐	hire a gardener and take all the credit

☐ ☐ ☐ wear a dirndl

☐ ☐ ☐ work as a poet in residence
at a college

☐ ☐ ☐ rock Twiggy-style eyelashes

☐ ☐ ☐ remain immune to beer goggles

☐ ☐ ☐ make pavlova

☐ ☐ ☐ watch a Muay Thai match in Thailand

☐ ☐ ☐ put bibliomancy to the test

☐ ☐ ☐ see Yngwie Malmsteen play live

☐ ☐ ☐ buy chunky turquoise jewellery

☐ ☐ ☐ identify as a dingledodie

☐ ☐ ☐ order an affogato for dessert

☐ ☐ ☐ explore Manjanggul Cave in South Korea

☐ ☐ ☐ wow someone with the factoid that koalas
aren't actually bears

☐ ☐ ☐ attend HonFest in Baltimore, Maryland

☐ ☐ ☐ try skijoring

☐ ☐ ☐ have your "only regret (be) not knowing what regret feels like"

☐ ☐ ☐ eat a chocolate crepe on the streets of Paris, France

☐ ☐ ☐ make a pitcher of agua fresca

☐ ☐ ☐ go to a Helmut Newton exhibit

☐ ☐ ☐ drink matcha instead of coffee

☐ ☐ ☐ give zero shits about visible panty lines

☐ ☐ ☐ find your tribe

☐ ☐ ☐ see the single remaining Wonder of the Ancient World

☐ ☐ ☐ see the Seven Wonders of the Modern World

☐ ☐ ☐ see the Seven Natural Wonders

☐ ☐ ☐ watch mumblecore movies

☐ ☐ ☐ forage for truffles with a trained hog

☐ ☐ ☐ slide into a celebrity's DMs and get a response

☐ ☐ ☐ train at the Iga Ninja School in Akame, Japan

bucket	f*ck it	done it	
☐	☐	☐	perform in a pantomime
☐	☐	☐	print pics instead of leaving them all on your phone
☐	☐	☐	use Aleppo soap
☐	☐	☐	play the Oregon Trail
☐	☐	☐	visit all nineteen Smithsonian museums
☐	☐	☐	skinny-dip
☐	☐	☐	help someone eliminate their vocal fry
☐	☐	☐	go to a vegan strip club in Portland, Oregon
☐	☐	☐	overshare with your barista and feel no shame
☐	☐	☐	trick someone with a fake pratfall
☐	☐	☐	read a book a week for a year
☐	☐	☐	order a ploughman's lunch at a pub
☐	☐	☐	dive down to a shipwreck
☐	☐	☐	visit Shackleton's Hut in Antarctica
☐	☐	☐	serenade a stranger

YOU HAVE DIED OF DYSENTERY. GAME OVER.

☐ ☐ ☐ groom a
French poodle

☐ ☐ ☐ throw a knuckleball

☐ ☐ ☐ celebrate the
Day of the Dead

☐ ☐ ☐ taste Turkish delight in Turkey

☐ ☐ ☐ work remotely

☐ ☐ ☐ listen to Polish reggae

☐ ☐ ☐ drink pumpkin wine

☐ ☐ ☐ watch Old Faithful erupt in Yellowstone
National Park in Wyoming

☐ ☐ ☐ commute via beach cruiser

☐ ☐ ☐ levitate

☐ ☐ ☐ do unto others as you would have others do
unto you (insert oral sex reference here)

☐ ☐ ☐ try ice blocking

☐ ☐ ☐ ride the high-speed Shinkansen in Japan

bucket	f*ck it	done it	
☐	☐	☐	write a memoir
☐	☐	☐	make a blood orange mimosa
☐	☐	☐	eat a barra burger in Australia
☐	☐	☐	stand on your head
☐	☐	☐	see a blue moon
☐	☐	☐	go to a concert at the Hollywood Forever Cemetery in Los Angeles, California
☐	☐	☐	do the fandango
☐	☐	☐	visit all of I. M. Pei's buildings
☐	☐	☐	practise tai chi
☐	☐	☐	hike in Samaria Gorge in Crete, Greece
☐	☐	☐	fall asleep to the sound of palm fronds swaying in the breeze
☐	☐	☐	watch episodes of *The Tonight Show* with Jimmy Fallon, Conan O'Brien, Jay Leno, and Johnny Carson and pick a favourite
☐	☐	☐	wear leather pants

☐☐☐ hop on a pogo stick

☐☐☐ change your name

☐☐☐ stay woke

☐☐☐ go noodling

☐☐☐ noodle on your guitar

☐☐☐ name all of the members of the Brat Pack

☐☐☐ name all of the members of the Rat Pack

☐☐☐ attend the Venice Film Festival in Italy

☐☐☐ get your eyebrows threaded

☐☐☐ run with the bulls in Pamplona, Spain

☐☐☐ leave a voicemail of your partner snoring on their phone so they know how bad it is

☐☐☐ eat a Baejarins Beztu Pylsur hot dog in Reykjavík, Iceland

☐☐☐ learn to speak German

☐☐☐ learn the difference between Swiss and Austrian German

bucket
f*ck it
done it

☐ ☐ ☐ roll your own sushi

☐ ☐ ☐ do the moonwalk

☐ ☐ ☐ consult an Ayurvedic doctor

☐ ☐ ☐ drink Cheerwine in North Carolina

☐ ☐ ☐ pose for Annie Leibovitz

☐ ☐ ☐ examine a bodily fluid under a
magnifying glass

☐ ☐ ☐ watch the Monaco Grand Prix

☐ ☐ ☐ spray someone with Silly String

☐ ☐ ☐ leave flowers on the Homomonument in
Amsterdam, Netherlands

☐ ☐ ☐ break through the glass ceiling

☐ ☐ ☐ meet a Trekkie

☐ ☐ ☐ make mayonnaise from scratch

☐ ☐ ☐ drum like Animal from *The Muppet Show*

☐ ☐ ☐ play the saxophone like Lisa from
The Simpsons

☐ ☐ ☐ figure out how to eat toffee without ripping out your fillings

☐ ☐ ☐ go commando

☐ ☐ ☐ play *sepak takraw*

☐ ☐ ☐ party at Amnesia in Ibiza, Spain

☐ ☐ ☐ count constellations at an International Dark Sky Park

☐ ☐ ☐ visit the town of Saint-Louis-du-Ha! Ha! in Quebec, Canada

☐ ☐ ☐ take up trainspotting

☐ ☐ ☐ listen to *bhangra* music

☐ ☐ ☐ date a ginger

☐ ☐ ☐ pick three desert island essentials

☐ ☐ ☐ surf in Lake Michigan

☐ ☐ ☐ go for *mezedes* and ouzo in Athens, Greece

☐ ☐ ☐ stay at the Grand Pupp Hotel in the Czech Republic

bucket	f*ck it	done it	

☐ ☐ ☐ book a flight around the world with frequent-flyer points

☐ ☐ ☐ eat beignets at Café du Monde in New Orleans, Louisiana

☐ ☐ ☐ look up at the Sugarloaf Mountain in Rio de Janeiro, Brazil

☐ ☐ ☐ play the tambourine in a band

☐ ☐ ☐ sniff lavender to help you sleep

☐ ☐ ☐ ferment your own sauerkraut

☐ ☐ ☐ read hardboiled fiction

☐ ☐ ☐ play the accordion

☐ ☐ ☐ go canyoning

☐ ☐ ☐ nerd out at Comic-Con

☐ ☐ ☐ open a beer bottle with your teeth

☐ ☐ ☐ pilgrimage to Graceland in Memphis, Tennessee

☐ ☐ ☐ describe something as Machiavellian

☐ ☐ ☐ ride the Cyclone at Coney Island in New York

☐ ☐ ☐ watch every episode of *Absolutely Fabulous*

☐ ☐ ☐ refer to yourself in the third person
for a day

☐ ☐ ☐ add an umlaut to your name

☐ ☐ ☐ drink Pocari Sweat

☐ ☐ ☐ play beer pong

HELLO
MY NAME IS
BÖB

☐ ☐ ☐ see a penguin in Patagonia

☐ ☐ ☐ use a mortar and pestle

☐ ☐ ☐ rush a frat

☐ ☐ ☐ rush a sorority

☐ ☐ ☐ hop on a colourful *chiva* bus in Colombia

☐ ☐ ☐ paint by numbers

☐ ☐ ☐ join a coven

☐ ☐ ☐ carry a flask

☐ ☐ ☐ see a play a day at the Fringe Festival in
Edinburgh, Scotland

☐ ☐ ☐ learn to love movies with subtitles

☐ ☐ ☐ grow heirloom tomatoes

☐ ☐ ☐ "get Schwifty"

☐ ☐ ☐ stop blaming millennials for everything

☐ ☐ ☐ ski the Body Bag run in Crested
Butte, Colorado

☐ ☐ ☐ do the hula

☐ ☐ ☐ create a signature barbecue sauce

☐ ☐ ☐ scan the surrounding countryside from a turret

☐ ☐ ☐ solve the mathematical Hodge conjecture

☐ ☐ ☐ pose for a pic with the Leaning Tower of Pisa,
making it look like you're holding it up

☐ ☐ ☐ foster a school garden project in
your neighbourhood

☐ ☐ ☐ believe in serendipity

☐ ☐ ☐ use the line "your name must be Wi-Fi, cos
I'm really feeling a connection"

☐ ☐ ☐ eat a bowl of bibimbap

☐ ☐ ☐ make a daisy chain

☐ ☐ ☐ explore the Mayan ruins of Xunantunich in San José Succotz, Belize

☐ ☐ ☐ hug Judah Friedlander

☐ ☐ ☐ examine your genitals with a hand mirror

☐ ☐ ☐ watch an elephant polo match in Rajasthan, India

☐ ☐ ☐ start a fake rumour to see how fast it spreads

☐ ☐ ☐ re-enact the beach make-out sesh from *From Here to Eternity*

☐ ☐ ☐ drink Horlicks and Ovaltine and pick a favourite

☐ ☐ ☐ see the world's largest totem pole in Alert Bay, Canada

☐ ☐ ☐ embrace your freckles

☐ ☐ ☐ call in sick to finish binge-watching
a show

☐ ☐ ☐ hit the bull's-eye and drop someone into the
dunk tank

☐ ☐ ☐ get invited to an asado in Argentina

☐ ☐ ☐ play baccarat

☐ ☐ ☐ keep a gratitude journal

☐ ☐ ☐ visit the town of Fucking, Austria

☐ ☐ ☐ match your outfit to your partner's every day
for a week

☐ ☐ ☐ dine at Chez Panisse in Berkeley, California

☐ ☐ ☐ try land yachting

☐ ☐ ☐ learn to tie an obi

☐ ☐ ☐ cruise the Danube

☐ ☐ ☐ co-opt the rhetoric (for good, not evil)

☐ ☐ ☐ listen to Kenyan hip-hop

☐ ☐ ☐ find the dark web

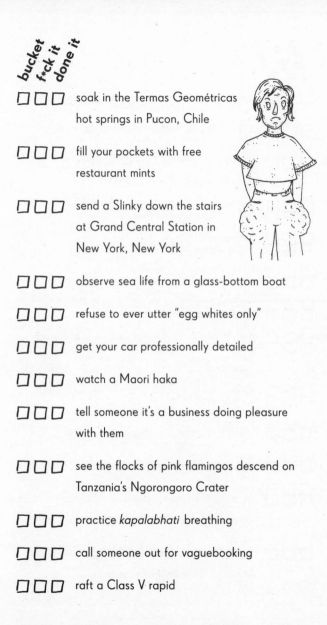

bucket
f*ck it
done it

☐ ☐ ☐ soak in the Termas Geométricas hot springs in Pucon, Chile

☐ ☐ ☐ fill your pockets with free restaurant mints

☐ ☐ ☐ send a Slinky down the stairs at Grand Central Station in New York, New York

☐ ☐ ☐ observe sea life from a glass-bottom boat

☐ ☐ ☐ refuse to ever utter "egg whites only"

☐ ☐ ☐ get your car professionally detailed

☐ ☐ ☐ watch a Maori haka

☐ ☐ ☐ tell someone it's a business doing pleasure with them

☐ ☐ ☐ see the flocks of pink flamingos descend on Tanzania's Ngorongoro Crater

☐ ☐ ☐ practice *kapalabhati* breathing

☐ ☐ ☐ call someone out for vaguebooking

☐ ☐ ☐ raft a Class V rapid

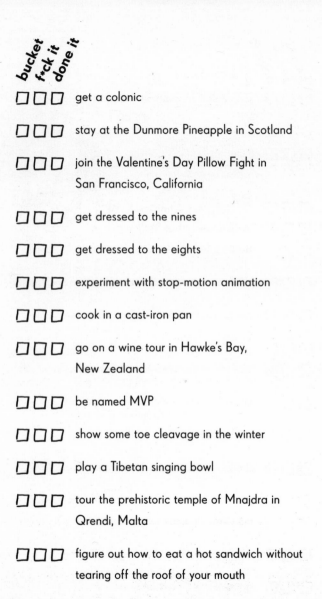

bucket
f*ck it
done it

☐ ☐ ☐ get a colonic

☐ ☐ ☐ stay at the Dunmore Pineapple in Scotland

☐ ☐ ☐ join the Valentine's Day Pillow Fight in
San Francisco, California

☐ ☐ ☐ get dressed to the nines

☐ ☐ ☐ get dressed to the eights

☐ ☐ ☐ experiment with stop-motion animation

☐ ☐ ☐ cook in a cast-iron pan

☐ ☐ ☐ go on a wine tour in Hawke's Bay,
New Zealand

☐ ☐ ☐ be named MVP

☐ ☐ ☐ show some toe cleavage in the winter

☐ ☐ ☐ play a Tibetan singing bowl

☐ ☐ ☐ tour the prehistoric temple of Mnajdra in
Qrendi, Malta

☐ ☐ ☐ figure out how to eat a hot sandwich without
tearing off the roof of your mouth

☐ ☐ ☐ be part of a live studio audience

☐ ☐ ☐ blow into a conch shell

☐ ☐ ☐ Smirnoff Ice someone

☐ ☐ ☐ study Greek mythology

☐ ☐ ☐ walk the Freedom Trail in
Boston, Massachusetts

☐ ☐ ☐ infiltrate Scientology and see what happens

☐ ☐ ☐ give in to verbal diarrhoea at Speakers'
Corner in London

☐ ☐ ☐ bite into a Carolina Reaper chilli pepper

☐ ☐ ☐ mend clothing instead of throwing it away

☐ ☐ ☐ study mycology

☐ ☐ ☐ drink a manhattan in Manhattan, New York

☐ ☐ ☐ practise self-care (insert masturbation
innuendo here)

☐ ☐ ☐ use mnemonics to improve your memory

☐ ☐ ☐ go rock crawling in a Jeep

☐ ☐ ☐ designate a day a week car-free

☐ ☐ ☐ eat buffalo milk ice cream

☐ ☐ ☐ visit Salvador Dalí's house in Port
Lligat, Spain

☐ ☐ ☐ try moxibustion therapy

☐ ☐ ☐ spot a grumble of pugs

☐ ☐ ☐ decorate with
Mexican oilcloth

☐ ☐ ☐ find Lasseter's Reef of gold in Australia

☐ ☐ ☐ watch all the *Sharknado* movies

☐ ☐ ☐ meet a Japanese Lolita

☐ ☐ ☐ buy a kilim

☐ ☐ ☐ see the Rai stones in Yap, Micronesia

☐ ☐ ☐ write a children's book

☐ ☐ ☐ swap your oven for an AGA

☐ ☐ ☐ master the Pelé-style bicycle soccer kick

☐ ☐ ☐ use a squat toilet without mishap

bucket
f*ck it
done it

☐ ☐ ☐ enter the O. Henry Pun-Off World Championships in Austin, Texas

☐ ☐ ☐ collect the entire Criterion Collection

☐ ☐ ☐ pretend to storm the ramparts of the fortified city of Carcassonne, France

☐ ☐ ☐ go roaming in the gloaming

☐ ☐ ☐ revive the saying "heavens to Murgatroyd"

☐ ☐ ☐ visit a pearl farm

☐ ☐ ☐ toss Mongolian *shagai* and learn your fortune

☐ ☐ ☐ drive the Merry Pranksters' bus route from La Honda, California, to New York, New York

☐ ☐ ☐ start a podcast

☐ ☐ ☐ drink rose petal wine

☐ ☐ ☐ take a public stance on Van Halen's David Lee Roth vs. Sammy Hagar

☐ ☐ ☐ live on a houseboat

☐ ☐ ☐ party at the Notting Hill Carnival

☐ ☐ ☐ party at Venice Carnival in Italy

☐ ☐ ☐ party at Mardi Gras in New Orleans, Louisiana

☐ ☐ ☐ party at the Carnival of Binche in Belgium

☐ ☐ ☐ party at the Provincetown Carnival in Massachusetts

☐ ☐ ☐ wear a bum bag ironically

☐ ☐ ☐ wear a bum bag unironically

☐ ☐ ☐ try telemarking

☐ ☐ ☐ eat a Scotch egg

☐ ☐ ☐ buy a Keane Eyes print

☐ ☐ ☐ start a Little Free Library

☐ ☐ ☐ train a therapy dog

☐ ☐ ☐ wear a Snuggie to work

☐ ☐ ☐ visit Skull Island and learn about head-hunting in the Solomon Islands

☐ ☐ ☐ watch a Cantonese opera

bucket
f*ck it
done it

☐ ☐ ☐ remain immune to the allure of the glitterati

☐ ☐ ☐ prove that penis envy is nothing but a fallacy

☐ ☐ ☐ see a gnu in the wild

☐ ☐ ☐ try rock balancing

☐ ☐ ☐ make your own mozzarella

☐ ☐ ☐ embrace your shiksappeal

☐ ☐ ☐ shop at the Pirate Supply Store in San Francisco, California

☐ ☐ ☐ have a diamond inset in your front tooth

☐ ☐ ☐ listen to whale songs

☐ ☐ ☐ role-play (for sexy times)

☐ ☐ ☑ role-play (for unsexy times)

☐ ☐ ☐ shuck oysters

☐ ☐ ☐ pick Jeju-do tangerines on Jeju Island, South Korea

☐ ☐ ☐   get hair extensions

☐ ☐ ☐   leave yourself a note in the bathroom every time you eat beetroot

☐ ☐ ☐   light a butter lamp in Tibet

☐ ☐ ☐   give a speech to more than a thousand people

☐ ☐ ☐   go to a flamenco bar in Seville, Spain

☐ ☐ ☐   sign up for a semester at sea

☐ ☐ ☐   keep your first business card as a reminder of how far you've come

☐ ☐ ☐   ogle the phalluses at a Japanese fertility shrine

☐ ☐ ☐   get cosy in a qiviut sweater

☐ ☐ ☐   find someone who actually likes fruit cake

☐ ☐ ☐   make it rain ... notes

☐ ☐ ☐   press flowers between the pages of an old book

☐ ☐ ☐   eat a Reuben sandwich in Omaha, Nebraska

☐ ☐ ☐   set up a bivouac

☐ ☐ ☐ watch a contortionist in action

☐ ☐ ☐ spend Groundhog Day in Punxsutawney, Pennsylvania

☐ ☐ ☐ go to mime school in Paris, France

☐ ☐ ☐ visit a butterfly aviary

☐ ☐ ☐ save a horse, ride a cowboy

☐ ☐ ☐ buy a Pucci scarf

☐ ☐ ☐ whittle

☐ ☐ ☐ drink Vietnamese coffee

☐ ☐ ☐ stop obsessing over your page views

☐ ☐ ☐ practise your breaststroke at the clothing-optional Yrjönkatu Swimming Hall in Helsinki, Finland

☐ ☐ ☐ attempt to make a seventeen-bird Rôti Sans Pareil

☐ ☐ ☐ get an action figure made in your likeness

155

☐ ☐ ☐ blush at the Museum of Sex in New York, New York

☐ ☐ ☐ catch the bouquet

☐ ☐ ☐ catch the garter

☐ ☐ ☐ restore a vintage car

☐ ☐ ☐ complete your magnum opus

☐ ☐ ☐ cheat death and eat fugu in Japan

☐ ☐ ☐ pierce your own ears

☐ ☐ ☐ do a keg stand

☐ ☐ ☐ sail past the entrance to Fingal's Cave in the Inner Hebrides, Scotland

☐ ☐ ☐ cure your own meats

☐ ☐ ☐ join a boxing club

☐ ☐ ☐ host an intellectual salon like in the days of yore

bucket
f*ck it
done it

☐ ☐ ☐ decide what your Patronus would be

☐ ☐ ☐ use your mother's maiden name – like Picasso

☐ ☐ ☐ cleverly disguise a case of swass

☐ ☐ ☐ attend the National Black Arts Festival in
Atlanta, Georgia

☐ ☐ ☐ hire a private detective

☐ ☐ ☐ eat a piece of Amish shoofly pie

☐ ☐ ☐ try urban exploring

☐ ☐ ☐ practise flair bartending (if you must)

☐ ☐ ☐ tour the Ksar of Ait-Ben-Haddou
in Morocco

☐ ☐ ☐ study the occult

☐ ☐ ☐ conduct an orchestra

☐ ☐ ☐ adopt a pet sugar glider

☐ ☐ ☐ drink port in Portugal

☐ ☐ ☐ watch a toilet flush in the opposite direction in
the Southern Hemisphere

☐ ☐ ☐   see a play at the Guthrie Theater in Minneapolis, Minnesota

☐ ☐ ☐   book a couple's massage on your anniversary

☐ ☐ ☐   ride a burro

☐ ☐ ☐   order *cendol* for dessert in Malaysia

☐ ☐ ☐   quote Neil deGrasse Tyson

☐ ☐ ☐   win a three-legged race

☐ ☐ ☐   sing "99 Bottles of Beer" the whole way through

☐ ☐ ☐   identify as a pogonophile

☐ ☐ ☐   go white-water kayaking

☐ ☐ ☐   eat strawberries and cream at Wimbledon

☐ ☐ ☐   plan to become an amateur Egyptologist when you retire

☐ ☐ ☐   wear a deerstalker hat

☐ ☐ ☐   mimic some of the Harlem Globetrotters' moves

☐ ☐ ☐ celebrate Purim

☐ ☐ ☐ manage to get a flattering
passport photo

☐ ☐ ☐ trim your own bangs

☐ ☐ ☐ start a wave at
a stadium

☐ ☐ ☐ read the book
before seeing
the movie

☐ ☐ ☐ boil your own bagels

☐ ☐ ☐ watch a marngrook match in Australia

☐ ☐ ☐ buy a Corvette without caring what people
say about your penis size

☐ ☐ ☐ run for mayor

☐ ☐ ☐ try *wire fu*

☐ ☐ ☐ win a moderated debate

☐ ☐ ☐ busk

bucket	f*ck it	done it	
☐	☐	☐	host a séance
☐	☐	☐	prove that the smell of the ocean is a balm for the soul
☐	☐	☐	ride the Deccan Odyssey train in India
☐	☐	☐	take a selfie with the Hollywood sign in the background
☐	☐	☐	bench-press more than your weight
☐	☐	☐	make a wish on a stray eyelash
☐	☐	☐	eat hairy crab in Shanghai, China
☐	☐	☐	accept that you have short arms and deep pockets
☐	☐	☐	practise *ubuntuism*
☐	☐	☐	taste your breast milk
☐	☐	☐	taste your partner's breast milk
☐	☐	☐	cruise the Mississippi

☐ ☐ ☐ create a cartoon character

☐ ☐ ☐ roll your own rugelach

☐ ☐ ☐ stroll through La Boca in Buenos Aires, Argentina

☐ ☐ ☐ play lacrosse

☐ ☐ ☐ stay in a house on stilts

☐ ☐ ☐ admit that you cried when Maverick threw Goose's dog tags in the water

☐ ☐ ☐ hear an owl hoot

☐ ☐ ☐ go to an oxygen bar

☐ ☐ ☐ hike the length of the Pacific Coast Trail

☐ ☐ ☐ attend the Tribeca Film Festival in New York, New York

☐ ☐ ☐ find a Pantone colour that matches your partner's eyes

☐ ☐ ☐ be able to identify every country's flag emoji

☐ ☐ ☐ chest bump

bucket	f*ck it	done it	
☐	☐	☐	join the Sourtoe Cocktail Club in Dawson City, Canada
☐	☐	☐	remember that sarcasm is the lowest form of wit and use it anyway
☐	☐	☐	discover the secret of the Bermuda Triangle
☐	☐	☐	listen to all of Beethoven's symphonies
☐	☐	☐	order an omelette at Lou Mitchell's in Chicago, Illinois
☐	☐	☐	watch an elaborate *rangoli* being made
☐	☐	☐	learn to raise one eyebrow coyly
☐	☐	☐	call someone "you old so-and-so"
☐	☐	☐	cycle to work every day for a week
☐	☐	☐	eat fresh guava
☐	☐	☐	make your own toothpaste
☐	☐	☐	wear leopard print from head to toe

☐ ☐ ☐ wear edible undies

☐ ☐ ☐ avoid getting Stendhal Syndrome at the Louvre in Paris, France

☐ ☐ ☐ watch a sea cucumber shoot its organs out of its anus

☐ ☐ ☐ get invited to a Swedish *fika*

☐ ☐ ☐ read all of Hunter S. Thompson's books

☐ ☐ ☐ brush a horse's mane

☐ ☐ ☐ look in the mirror and say "Bloody Mary" three times

☐ ☐ ☐ drink a pisco sour in Peru

☐ ☐ ☐ eat rabbit at Easter

☐ ☐ ☐ witness cowrie shell divination

☐ ☐ ☐ throw a shot put

☐ ☐ ☐ throw a discus

☐ ☐ ☐ throw a hammer

☐ ☐ ☐ grill fruit on your barbecue

☐ ☐ ☐ refuse to kowtow to conformity

☐ ☐ ☐ go on a gorilla trek in Virunga National Park in the Congo

☐ ☐ ☐ give a bravura performance

☐ ☐ ☐ master noseriding

☐ ☐ ☐ attend a murder mystery dinner

☐ ☐ ☐ eat a spoonful of lentils on New Year's Eve after midnight for luck in the coming year

☐ ☐ ☐ stay at the Steel Magnolia House B&B in Natchitoches, Louisiana

☐ ☐ ☐ collect orchids

☐ ☐ ☐ learn the difference between a *maiko* and a geisha

☐ ☐ ☐ watch a bus-pulling competition

☐ ☐ ☐ summit Ben Nevis in Scotland

☐ ☐ ☐ study Tibetan mythology

☐ ☐ ☐ tour Iolani Palace in Honolulu, Hawaii

☐ ☐ ☐ meet your favourite celebrity chef

☐ ☐ ☐ hear the Boston Pops live

☐ ☐ ☐ chew kola nuts

☐ ☐ ☐ try auriculotherapy

☐ ☐ ☐ watch a water puppet performance in Hanoi, Vietnam

☐ ☐ ☐ find a cure for affluenza

☐ ☐ ☐ use a menstrual cup instead of pads or tampons

☐ ☐ ☐ decorate your house to look like a Wes Anderson movie

☐ ☐ ☐ BASE jump

☐ ☐ ☐ triumph over a claw machine and win a toy

☐ ☐ ☐ admire the *alebrije* in Oaxaca, Mexico

☐ ☐ ☐ complete the Dublin City Liffey Swim in Ireland

☐ ☐ ☐ eat a chicken named Colin

THE CLAW

☐ ☐ ☐ use a wine aroma kit

☐ ☐ ☐ organise a house exchange

☐ ☐ ☐ keep track of the shit your dad says

☐ ☐ ☐ admire the art deco buildings in Miami, Florida

☐ ☐ ☐ follow the Meisner technique of acting

☐ ☐ ☐ sport a blunt bob

☐ ☐ ☐ see the female Van Halen tribute band
Vag Halen in concert

☐ ☐ ☐ climb the red sand dunes in Namib-Naukluft
National Park in Namibia

☐ ☐ ☐ email your local supermarket suggesting
a cookie butter-flavoured lube

☐ ☐ ☐ plant a bee-friendly garden

☐ ☐ ☐ convert to a
different religion

FOR YOUR PLEASURE
COOKIE
BUTTER
LUBE

☐ ☐ ☐ go to an EDM festival

☐ ☐ ☐ consult a witch doctor

☐ ☐ ☐ buy a batik in Bali, Indonesia

☐ ☐ ☐ visit the Anne of Green Gables farmhouse in Cavendish, Canada

☐ ☐ ☐ pick fruit from trees on public land

☐ ☐ ☐ watch a Taos Hoop Dance in New Mexico

☐ ☐ ☐ play ice hockey

☐ ☐ ☐ play field hockey

☐ ☐ ☐ see a Spanish Dildo Cactus at the Guánica Biosphere Reserve in Puerto Rico

☐ ☐ ☐ demystify someone's superstition for them

☐ ☐ ☐ make ramen in a coffeepot

☐ ☐ ☐ vote with your dollars

☐ ☐ ☐ skip out on a gender reveal party

☐ ☐ ☐ use a banana peel to shine your shoes

☐ ☐ ☐ enter a shin-kicking competition in the Cotswold Olimpick Games

☐ ☐ ☐ learn the NATO alphabet

bucket
f*ck it
done it

☐ ☐ ☐ celebrate Galentine's Day with your BFF

☐ ☐ ☐ write a pangram sentence

☐ ☐ ☐ check the Vegas odds on your team winning
the Super Bowl

☐ ☐ ☐ experience *la douleur exquise*

☐ ☐ ☐ ride shotgun in a hearse

☐ ☐ ☐ see the Great Wall of China

☐ ☐ ☐ eat saltwater taffy on the Jersey Shore

☐ ☐ ☐ count the number of licks it takes to get to the
Tootsie Roll centre of a Tootsie Pop

☐ ☐ ☐ play the bagpipes

☐ ☐ ☐ host a raclette party

☐ ☐ ☐ draw fashion inspiration
from Grace Jones

☐ ☐ ☐ go mountain running

☐ ☐ ☐ strive to be a DINK
(dual income no kids)

☐ ☐ ☐ throw a ninja star

☐ ☐ ☐ drink at Ozone on the 118th floor of the Ritz-Carlton, Hong Kong, China

☐ ☐ ☐ write a letter to a younger version of yourself

☐ ☐ ☐ keep a stash of greeting cards in your desk — just in case

☐ ☐ ☐ learn to speak Urdu

☐ ☐ ☐ fillet a fish

☐ ☐ ☐ make cinnamon toast for breakfast

☐ ☐ ☐ meet a coulrophile

☐ ☐ ☐ climb up the stairs of the ancient fortress of Sigiriya in Sri Lanka

☐ ☐ ☐ stroll under the Spanish moss

☐ ☐ ☐ park by the runway and watch the planes take off

☐ ☐ ☐ streak at a sporting event

☐ ☐ ☐ watch the Mummers Parade in Philadelphia, Pennsylvania

169

☐ ☐ ☐ sleep in a Navajo hogan

☐ ☐ ☐ soak in a milk bath

☐ ☐ ☐ film a documentary

☐ ☐ ☐ eat at a *dhaba* along the Silk Road

☐ ☐ ☐ embrace the hurly-burly

☐ ☐ ☐ indulge in a *shirodhara* treatment

☐ ☐ ☐ memorise a monologue

☐ ☐ ☐ tell an a cappella group they are
"aca-awesome"

☐ ☐ ☐ take a sabbatical

☐ ☐ ☐ skip a stone across the water

☐ ☐ ☐ play pickleball

☐ ☐ ☐ try the phallic Soup No. 5 in the Philippines

☐ ☐ ☐ do the Dougie

☐ ☐ ☐ learn to speed-read

☐ ☐ ☐ perfect your pyrography technique

☐ ☐ ☐ buy a 3-D printer

☐ ☐ ☐ check the time on the Prague Astronomical
Clock in the Czech Republic

☐ ☐ ☐ snowboard in Whistler, British Columbia,
Canada

☐ ☐ ☐ sear fish on a block of Himalayan salt

☐ ☐ ☐ join the Explorers Club

☐ ☐ ☐ tie an Eldredge knot

☐ ☐ ☐ go on a wine tour in Adelaide Hills in Australia

☐ ☐ ☐ see an orca in the wild

☐ ☐ ☐ organise a treasure hunt

☐ ☐ ☐ put the "fun" in
dysfunction at your
next family dinner

☐ ☐ ☐ blow a bubblegum
bubble bigger than your head

☐ ☐ ☐ walk through Red Square in Moscow, Russia

☐ ☐ ☐ witness telekinesis

☐ ☐ ☐ consult a doctor of Chinese medicine

☐ ☐ ☐ draw fashion inspiration from Liberace

☐ ☐ ☐ take your bra off through your sleeve
Flashdance -style

☐ ☐ ☐ eat a Cornish pasty

☐ ☐ ☐ dry brush daily

☐ ☐ ☐ follow your bliss

☐ ☐ ☐ drink cashew *feni* in Goa, India

☐ ☐ ☐ see the Bonneville Salt Flats in Utah

☐ ☐ ☐ go to an Andrew Lloyd Webber musical

☐ ☐ ☐ grow your own herbs

☐ ☐ ☐ visit Persepolis in Iran

☐ ☐ ☐ play strip poker

☐ ☐ ☐ buy an Eames
lounge chair

☐ ☐ ☐ smell the rotting
meat-scented stink lily

☐ ☐ ☐ assume a mysterious-sounding alias

☐ ☐ ☐ stop eating sugar

☐ ☐ ☐ jet boat through the Shotover River canyons in New Zealand

☐ ☐ ☐ start a petition

☐ ☐ ☐ adopt a monochromatic aesthetic

☐ ☐ ☐ boulder a V10

☐ ☐ ☐ pillage your parents' record collection

☐ ☐ ☐ wear a cocktail ring

☐ ☐ ☐ investigate a conspiracy theory

☐ ☐ ☐ meet a furry

☐ ☐ ☐ listen to Swedish hip-hop

☐ ☐ ☐ walk across the Golden Gate Bridge in San Francisco, California

☐ ☐ ☐ watch all of the Coen Brother movies

☐ ☐ ☐ stop hate-following people on Instagram

☐ ☐ ☐ see a charm of goldfinches

☐ ☐ ☐   have an orgasmic birth

☐ ☐ ☐   learn the difference between primary, secondary, and tertiary colours

☐ ☐ ☐   be unapologetically bougie

☐ ☐ ☐   read the entire *Dragon Ball* manga series

☐ ☐ ☐   drink the fecal *kopi luwak* coffee

☐ ☐ ☐   try *dødsing* in Norway

☐ ☐ ☐   use breath spray on a date

☐ ☐ ☐   make a *kokedama* planter

☐ ☐ ☐   ride the Golden Horn Ferry in Istanbul, Turkey

☐ ☐ ☐   sign up to be a Nielsen's Ratings Family

☐ ☐ ☐   explore the Palm Jumeirah in Dubai, United Arab Emirates

☐ ☐ ☐   attend the James Beard Awards Gala

☐ ☐ ☐   nap in a hayloft

☐ ☐ ☐   find out why the word "moist" is so disgusting

☐ ☐ ☐ watch spring training in Arizona

☐ ☐ ☐ watch spring training
in Florida

☐ ☐ ☐ play Quidditch

☐ ☐ ☐ tap-dance

☐ ☐ ☐ make eggs and soldiers
for breakfast

☐ ☐ ☐ get the hang of adulting

☐ ☐ ☐ reread your adolescent diary without cringing

☐ ☐ ☐ go on a pub crawl

☐ ☐ ☐ live in a penthouse

☐ ☐ ☐ walk on the wings of a biplane

☐ ☐ ☐ drink moon milk to help you sleep

☐ ☐ ☐ eat Fig Newtons in Newton, Massachusetts

☐ ☐ ☐ hoop dance

☐ ☐ ☐ play snooker

☐ ☐ ☐ meditate every day for a month

bucket
f*ck it
done it

☐☐☐ meet a dog that won Best in Show at Crufts

☐☐☐ wear a mantilla

☐☐☐ celebrate Steak and Blowjob Day

☐☐☐ join a Critical Mass bike ride

☐☐☐ stay in Delhi and avoid getting Delhi Belly

☐☐☐ run off the end of a dock into a lake

☐☐☐ raft the Magpie River in Ontario, Canada

☐☐☐ snack on salmon candy

☐☐☐ listen to Menudo

☐☐☐ light one of your farts on fire

☐☐☐ sail to Catalina Island in California

☐☐☐ become a foe to mediocrity

☐☐☐ buy a map and colour in all the countries you've visited

☐☐☐ make a pitcher of sangria

☐☐☐ sit on the Iron Throne

☐ ☐ ☐ use the perfume samples in magazines
instead of buying a bottle

☐ ☐ ☐ watch the Man versus Horse Marathon
in Llanwrtyd Wells, Wales

☐ ☐ ☐ pat your head and rub your
stomach at the same time

☐ ☐ ☐ see a narwhal in the wild

☐ ☐ ☐ create your own sigil

☐ ☐ ☐ jazz up your cheese plate with a slab of
honeycomb, fresh figs, and frozen grapes

☐ ☐ ☐ see your name in lights

☐ ☐ ☐ recognise onomatopoeia when you hear it

☐ ☐ ☐ eat a Barbados cutter

☐ ☐ ☐ compete in the Air Sex World Championships

☐ ☐ ☐ take out your frustrations at a driving range

☐ ☐ ☐ charter a plane

☐ ☐ ☐ stay at Nishiyama Onsen Keiunkan in Japan –
the oldest hotel in the world

☐ ☐ ☐ try baton twirling

☐ ☐ ☐ crack a code

☐ ☐ ☑ pace yourself and don't eat all of your Advent
calendar in one sitting

☐ ☐ ☐ tell someone you know "a load of codswallop
when you hear one"

☐ ☐ ☑ walk the High Line in New York, New York

☐ ☐ ☐ create an IMDb profile

☐ ☐ ☐ play squash

☐ ☐ ☐ unearth an old Atari and play Pong

☐ ☐ ☐ work as a seat filler at the Oscars

☐ ☐ ☐ visit Shakespeare's birthplace in
Stratford-upon-Avon

☐ ☐ ☐ see Four Corners – where Arizona,
New Mexico, Utah, and Colorado meet

☐ ☐ ☐ try parasailing

☐ ☐ ☐ backpack around Europe

bucket
f*ck it
done it

☐ ☐ ☐ find the perfect music festival outfit

☐ ☐ ☐ go to Coachella in Indio, California

☐ ☐ ☐ go to Bonnaroo in Manchester, Tennessee

☐ ☐ ☐ go to Glastonbury

☐ ☐ ☐ go to Splendour in the Grass near Byron Bay,
        New South Wales, Australia

☐ ☐ ☐ go to Fuji Rock Festival in Niigata
        Prefecture, Japan

☐ ☐ ☐ drink snake wine

☐ ☐ ☐ travel by pirogue

☐ ☐ ☑ salivate over something

☐ ☐ ☐ choose a signature drink

☐ ☐ ☐ choose a signature scent

☐ ☐ ☐ join a community group

☐ ☐ ☐ go to a cat café

□ □ □ experience brain freeze and
orgasm simultaneously

□ □ □ find out if "Moves like Jagger" has something
to do with Marianne Faithfull and a Mars bar

□ □ □ tip the toilet attendant generously

□ □ □ leave a trail of glitter wherever you go

□ □ □ visit the *Titanic* burial grounds in Halifax,
Nova Scotia

□ □ □ build a ship in a bottle

□ □ □ play the tabla

□ □ □ eat black sapote fruit and see if it tastes like
chocolate pudding

□ □ □ add a *marimo* to your
plant collection

□ □ □ drive a vintage
Volkswagen van

□ □ □ try toe wrestling

□ □ □ watch the Palm Desert
Golf Cart Parade in Palm Desert, California

☐ ☐ ☐ experience sound healing

☐ ☐ ☐ run and drink at the Marathon du Médoc in France

☐ ☐ ☐ heed the lessons from *Aesop's Fables*

☐ ☐ ☐ be mindful of people's triggers

☐ ☐ ☐ attempt the 100-Mile Diet

☐ ☐ ☐ quote Yoda

☐ ☐ ☐ dig up geoduck on the Oregon coast

☐ ☐ ☐ photobomb a celebrity

☐ ☐ ☐ have a celebrity photobomb you

☐ ☐ ☐ visit the town of Å in Norway

☐ ☐ ☐ bake Mexican wedding cookies

☐ ☐ ☐ compost

☐ ☐ ☐ watch the *falla* figures burn at the Feast of Saint Joseph in Valencia, Spain

☐ ☐ ☐ order a custom hood ornament for your car

☐ ☐ ☐ commute via skateboard

☐ ☐ ☐ taste manuka honey

☐ ☐ ☐ play solitaire with cards instead of on a computer

☐ ☐ ☐ hang a colourful *pajaki* chandelier in your house

☐ ☐ ☐ figure out what your real-life MacGuffin is

☐ ☐ ☐ gather your cojones and eat *casu marzu* in Sardinia, Italy

☐ ☐ ☐ boycott Sea World

☐ ☐ ☐ wear a gold grill

☐ ☐ ☐ get a personalised number plate

☐ ☐ ☐ watch a Balinese dance performance

☐ ☐ ☐ walk away when someone makes air quotes as they talk

☐ ☐ ☐ attempt to revive the lost art of letter writing

☐ ☐ ☐ make out at a drive-in movie

☐ ☐ ☐ see Ale's Stones in Sweden

bucket
f*ck it
done it

☐ ☐ ☐ plant a tree every year on Earth Day

☐ ☐ ☐ do a two-person cartwheel

☐ ☐ ☐ memorise all the words to every song in *Rent*

☐ ☐ ☐ visit Petra in Jordan

☐ ☐ ☐ try welly wanging

☐ ☐ ☐ do a gumboot dance

☐ ☐ ☐ surf at Playa Guiones in Costa Rica

☐ ☐ ☐ go mudflat hiking in the Netherlands

☐ ☐ ☐ ask a German if *pumpernickel* really means "devil's fart"

☐ ☐ ☐ take the Myers-Briggs test

☐ ☐ ☐ suppress your primeval urge to dance whenever "YMCA" comes on

bucket it
f*ck it
done it

□ □ □ pose for a picture with Big Pineapple in Queensland, Australia

□ □ □ identify as an aesthete

□ □ □ make a divining rod

□ □ □ try dousing

□ □ □ go to Waikiki Spam Jam Festival in Honolulu, Hawaii

□ □ □ rewatch your school leavers' speech ten years after graduation

□ □ □ ride in a glider

□ □ □ drag race

□ □ □ watch every single episode of *RuPaul's Drag Race*

□ □ □ visit Voudou Queen Priestess Marie Laveau's grave in New Orleans, Louisiana

□ □ □ eat neeps and tatties

□ □ □ see a platypus in the wild

□ □ □ embrace hedonism

☐ ☐ ☐ pluck a flower's petals to see if they love you or love you not

☐ ☐ ☐ go inside an Iban longhouse in Sarawak, Borneo

☐ ☐ ☐ dedicate a park bench in someone's honour

☐ ☐ ☐ drink a Bellini at Harry's Bar in Venice, Italy

☐ ☐ ☐ work as a roadie and tour the country

☐ ☐ ☐ soak in the Yangpachen Hot Springs in Tibet

☐ ☐ ☐ move into the corner office

☐ ☐ ☐ send someone a dik-dik pic

☐ ☐ ☐ host a monthly board game night

☐ ☐ ☐ write a think piece on *Road House*

☐ ☐ ☐ boogie board

☐ ☐ ☐ walk the length of the Coast to Coast Walkway in Auckland, New Zealand

☐ ☐ ☐ tag along with a group of storm chasers

bucket
f*ck it
done it

☐ ☐ ☐ install a skylight above your bed

☐ ☐ ☐ buy a copy of your favourite book for all of your friends

☐ ☐ ☐ practise astral projection

☐ ☐ ☐ party at Crazy Horse in Paris, France

☐ ☐ ☐ visit the Crazy Horse Memorial in South Dakota

☐ ☐ ☐ tend to your playlists as you would your plants

☐ ☐ ☐ understand the Filipino concept of *bahala na*

☐ ☐ ☐ play the harp

☐ ☐ ☐ give someone goose bumps

☐ ☐ ☐ land an internship at your dream company

☐ ☐ ☐ collect restaurant matchbooks

☐ ☐ ☐ eat a Cuban sandwich in Miami, Florida

☐ ☐ ☐ cheer for anyone except Real Madrid

☐ ☐ ☐ krump

☐ ☐ ☐ use a *nazar* to ward off the evil eye

☐ ☐ ☐ enter the Iditarod Trail Sled Dog Race in Alaska

☐ ☐ ☐ enter the Idiotarod in New York, New York

☐ ☐ ☐ leave the "Do Not Disturb" sign up all day

☐ ☐ ☐ brazenly wear white after Labor Day

☐ ☐ ☐ stay at Giraffe Manor in Nairobi, Kenya

☐ ☐ ☐ start using the word "tomfoolery"

☐ ☐ ☐ tour the Good Vibrations Antique Vibrator Museum in San Francisco, California

☐ ☐ ☐ buy cookies by the case from Brownies

☐ ☐ ☐ culture jam

☐ ☐ ☐ sport a finger wave hairdo

☐ ☐ ☐ throw a dart at a map and go where it lands

☐ ☐ ☐ use an old-fashioned butter churn

☐ ☐ ☐ eat mochi

☐ ☐ ☐ recreate a runway look for less

☐ ☐ ☐ go in the Gellért Hill Cave Church in Budapest, Hungary

☐ ☐ ☐ bobsled

☐ ☐ ☐ play the bongos naked à la Matthew McConaughey

☐ ☐ ☐ train as a smoke jumper

☐ ☐ ☐ spin a prayer wheel

☐ ☐ ☐ visit the Montezuma Castle National Monument in Arizona

☐ ☐ ☐ go downhill mountain biking

☐ ☐ ☐ wear a heart-monitor during sex

☐ ☐ ☐ sport a walrus moustache

☐ ☐ ☐ adopt a low-maintenance brush and flush bedtime routine

☐ ☐ ☐ watch the Singapore Grand Prix

☐ ☐ ☐ make a savoury aspic

☐ ☐ ☐ play Black Sabbath backwards and listen for hidden messages

☐ ☐ ☐ drink tequila, mezcal, pulque, *raicilla,* and *bacanora* and pick a favourite

☐ ☐ ☐ refuse to fall prey to tall poppy syndrome

☐ ☐ ☐ go to a show at the Apollo Theater in Harlem, New York

☐ ☐ ☐ eat Nepalese *momos*

☐ ☐ ☐ grow a moustache and support Movember

☐ ☐ ☐ meet a paranormal investigator

☐ ☐ ☐ harvest salt on Salt Island in the British Virgin Islands

☐ ☐ ☐ throw a little salt over your shoulder for good luck

☐ ☐ ☐ silence your critics

☐ ☐ ☐ shout *"opa"* at a Greek celebration

☐ ☐ ☐ make Eton mess for dessert

☐ ☐ ☐ visit the Tiger's Nest Monastery in Bhutan

☐ ☐ ☐ attempt the Fosbury Flop

☐ ☐ ☐ breathe deeply through turbulence –
aeronautical or otherwise

☐ ☐ ☐ try reflexology

☐ ☐ ☐ get cosy in a Hudson's Bay Company blanket

☐ ☐ ☐ attend the Bellybutton Festival in
Furano, Japan

☐ ☐ ☐ put the kibosh on baby talk

☐ ☐ ☐ buy a summerhouse

☐ ☐ ☐ settle a dispute with a dance-off

☐ ☐ ☐ tour the haunted Winchester Mystery House
in San Jose, California

☐ ☐ ☐ play water polo

☐ ☐ ☐ climb the ornate Caltagirone staircase in
Sicily, Italy

☐ ☐ ☐ wear a fedora and not look like a douche

☐ ☐ ☐ have a body part insured

☐ ☐ ☐ use rose quartz to heal a broken heart

☐ ☐ ☐ learn Morse code

☐ ☐ ☐ buy only non-GM foods

☐ ☐ ☐ eat ackee in Jamaica

☐ ☐ ☐ join a Tweed Run

☐ ☐ ☐ date a Suicide Girl

☐ ☐ ☐ date a bear

☐ ☐ ☐ volunteer at a soup kitchen

☐ ☐ ☐ bite off the ends of a piece of liquorice and use it as a straw

☐ ☐ ☐ join the 50 States Marathon Club

☐ ☐ ☐ get lucky in Kentucky

☐ ☐ ☐ watch a *pehlwani* wrestling match

☐ ☐ ☐ take a class at the Institute of Brewing and Distilling in London

☐ ☐ ☐ spin a bull-roarer

☐ ☐ ☐ debate auteur theory

☐☐☐ master the Alaskan high kick

☐☐☐ make purple potato salad

☐☐☐ go on a social media fast for a week

☐☐☐ work the pottery wheel
Ghost-style

☐☐☐ ride the Indian Pacific train
from Sydney to Perth
in Australia

☐☐☐ get your makeup
professionally done

☐☐☐ stay single during cuffing season

☐☐☐ see a Junkanoo parade in the Bahamas

☐☐☐ watch *Attack of the Killer Tomatoes*

☐☐☐ make an anatomically correct snowman

☐☐☐ visit the Chicken Church in Java, Indonesia

☐☐☐ have a conversation using only song lyrics

☐☐☐ eat at a *gastätte, eiscafé, ratskeller, bierkeller,*
and *imbiss* in Germany

☐ ☐ ☐ wear a GoPro while giving birth

☐ ☐ ☐ craft with *washi* tape

☐ ☐ ☐ memorise all of the bones in the human body

☐ ☐ ☐ show off your *mehndi*

☐ ☐ ☐ teach someone what Tribeca and Soho are short for

☐ ☐ ☐ drive across the Hoover Dam

☐ ☐ ☐ decide to start beefing up your obituary now

☐ ☐ ☐ live in a converted shipping container

☐ ☐ ☐ rock climb in Railay, Thailand

☐ ☐ ☐ attend the Hong Kong Film Festival in China

☐ ☐ ☐ name your partner's genitals

☐ ☐ ☐ become a tenured professor

☐ ☐ ☐ indulge in a *watsu* massage

☐ ☐ ☐ go heli-skiing

☐ ☐ ☐ furnish your house with items from the "free" section of Craigslist

☐ ☐ ☐ ponder existentialism at Les Deux Magots in Paris, France

☐ ☐ ☐ wear pink on Wednesdays

☐ ☐ ☐ eat at Whoopi Goldburger in Tokyo, Japan

☐ ☐ ☐ make a tiny devilled quail egg

☐ ☐ ☐ make a giant devilled ostrich egg

☐ ☐ ☐ see the original *Fargo* wood chipper at the Visitor Center in Fargo, North Dakota

☐ ☐ ☐ listen to the Queen's speech every Christmas

☐ ☐ ☐ spice a recipe with *gomasio*

☐ ☐ ☐ buy the tackiest souvenir you can find while on holiday

☐ ☐ ☐ get a traditional tattoo

☐ ☐ ☐ pilgrimage to Bon Scott's grave in Freemantle, Australia

bucket	f*ck it	done it

☐ ☐ ☐ talk someone out of their comb-over

☐ ☐ ☐ start using the word "frisson"
when you're excited

☐ ☐ ☐ tool some leather

☐ ☐ ☐ get your makeup
tattooed on

☐ ☐ ☐ watch the Hasty Pudding Theatricals crown
their Man and Woman of the Year

☐ ☐ ☐ overhear someone refer to you as a polymath

☐ ☐ ☐ visit the Haghpat and Sanahin monasteries
in Armenia

☐ ☐ ☐ use the line "if you were words on a page,
you'd be fine print"

☐ ☐ ☐ play shogi

☐ ☐ ☐ tube down the Nam Song River in
Vang Vieng, Laos

☐ ☐ ☐ reply to one of your boss's emails with "tl;dr"

☐ ☐ ☐ drink Lester's Fixins Ranch Dressing Soda

bucket	f*ck it	done it	
☐	☐	☐	try cupping therapy
☐	☐	☐	sit on the world's longest porch at the Grand Hotel on Mackinac Island, Michigan
☐	☐	☐	climb the Grouse Grind in North Vancouver, Canada
☐	☐	☐	see a cock of the rock in the wild
☐	☐	☐	learn to say "I love you" in five different languages
☐	☐	☐	practise primordial sound meditation
☐	☐	☐	eat pink Radicchio del Veneto lettuce in Italy
☐	☐	☐	study phrenology
☐	☐	☐	leave a dog biscuit on Toto's grave in Los Angeles, California
☐	☐	☐	listen to all of the BBC Sessions albums
☐	☐	☐	visit the Velveteria museum in Los Angeles, California

bucket	f*ck it	done it	
☐	☐	☐	admit that you didn't like *The Catcher in the Rye*
☐	☐	☐	convince someone that a female peacock is a peacunt
☐	☐	☐	walk along Cannon Beach in Oregon
☐	☐	☐	whisk someone away for a romantical weekend
☐	☐	☐	buy a Wenger Giant Swiss Army Knife and use all eighty-five of its tools
☐	☐	☐	sunbathe on the roof of your building
☐	☐	☐	use fresh wasabi instead of powdered
☐	☐	☐	cruise the Yangtze
☐	☐	☐	bodysurf
☐	☐	☐	mic drop
☐	☐	☐	see the Grand Canyon
☐	☐	☐	watch an otter relaxing on its back
☐	☐	☐	look up at the Soufrière Hills volcano in Montserrat

☐ ☐ ☐ carry a trident around and see what happens

☐ ☐ ☐ visit all of Zaha Hadid's buildings

☐ ☐ ☐ drink every time someone says "one lucky buyer" or "later in the programme" on *Homes Under the Hammer*

☐ ☐ ☐ eat poi and tell people it is "poi-fect"

☐ ☐ ☐ eschew pragmatism

☐ ☐ ☐ play a round at the grassless One Boat Golf Club on Ascension Island

☐ ☐ ☐ go ATVing

☐ ☐ ☐ enter a watermelon seed-spitting contest

☐ ☐ ☐ learn to speak Mi'kmaq

☐ ☐ ☐ wear a locket around your neck with pics of your pets in it

☐ ☐ ☐ gongoozle

☐ ☐ ☐ drink Turkish coffee

☐ ☐ ☐ milk a cow

☐ ☐ ☐ explore the Meramec Caverns in Missouri

☐ ☐ ☐ make a life-size replica of something
with Lego

☐ ☐ ☐ watch *This Is Spinal Tap* and turn it up to 11

☐ ☐ ☐ stay at a love hotel in Japan

☐ ☐ ☐ find out if you're also allergic to cats if you're
allergic to lions

☐ ☐ ☐ describe something as Orwellian

☐ ☐ ☐ use a Muffpot to sled cook a meal

☐ ☐ ☐ explore the Shawshank Trail in and around
Mansfield, Ohio

☐ ☐ ☐ enter a snow volleyball tournament

☐ ☐ ☐ windsurf

bucket	f*ck it	done it	
☐	☐	☐	support the Apostrophe Protection Society
☐	☐	☐	visit the village of Nether Wallop, England
☐	☐	☐	march to help Take Back the Night
☐	☐	☐	spot the official bird of Redondo Beach, California — the Goodyear Blimp
☐	☐	☐	ride in a submarine
☐	☐	☐	live in a house with a name rather than a numerical address
☐	☐	☐	suggest a moratorium on Kilner jars
☐	☐	☐	name your boat after the person you lost your virginity to
☐	☐	☐	dip your toes in the Java Sea
☐	☐	☐	walk on the roof of the Oslo Opera House in Norway
☐	☐	☐	go thru-hiking
☐	☐	☐	watch *Ocean's 11* from 1960 and *Ocean's Eleven* from 2001 and pick a favourite
☐	☐	☐	jump off the high dive without hesitation

☐ ☐ ☐ collect colourful Depression glassware

☐ ☐ ☐ cast a spell

☐ ☐ ☐ pickle your own pickles

☐ ☐ ☐ wear chaps

☐ ☐ ☐ offer someone a moustache ride

☐ ☐ ☐ crash the Met Gala in
New York, New York

☐ ☐ ☐ listen to ripsaw music in
Turks and Caicos

☐ ☐ ☐ try on a traditional Korean *hanbok*

☐ ☐ ☐ take the LSAT just to see how you do

☐ ☐ ☐ happen upon a jazzfuneral in
New Orleans, Louisiana

☐ ☐ ☐ see the rock-hewn churches in
Lalibela, Ethiopia

☐ ☐ ☐ adopt a noblesse oblige outlook

☐ ☐ ☐ drink a Dutch *kopstootje*

☐ ☐ ☐ eat burdock

☐ ☐ ☐ walk a labyrinth

☐ ☐ ☐ join a dodgeball league

☐ ☐ ☐ put up a Charlie Brown Christmas tree

☐ ☐ ☐ go to a Takashi Murakami exhibit

☐ ☐ ☐ find a fulgurite after a lightning storm

☐ ☐ ☐ attend a *Dirty Dancing*-themed weekend at the Mountain Lake Lodge in Pembroke, Virginia

☐ ☐ ☐ identify as a doyenne

☐ ☐ ☐ watch Italian neorealism films

☐ ☐ ☐ see the pink slugs of Mount Kaputar, Australia

☐ ☐ ☐ tour the flavour graveyard at the Ben & Jerry's factory in Waterbury, Vermont

☐ ☐ ☐ champion on behalf of the SarcMark punctuation mark

☐ ☐ ☐ dress in head-to-toe red during your period

☐ ☐ ☐ explore the Alnwick Poison Garden

☐ ☐ ☐ invent a way to clean up the Great Pacific Garbage Patch

☐ ☐ ☐ try wingsuit flying

☐ ☐ ☐ choreograph an elaborate lip dub

☐ ☐ ☐ draw fashion inspiration from André 3000

☐ ☐ ☐ ride the House on the Rock carousel in Wisconsin

☐ ☐ ☐ flip through your school yearbook without cringing

☐ ☐ ☐ sign up to be an organ donor

☐ ☐ ☐ try a new recipe every week for a year

☐ ☐ ☐ stand over a vent in a dress à la Marilyn Monroe

☐ ☐ ☐ explore the remains of Urquhart Castle on the shores of Loch Ness, Scotland

☐ ☐ ☐ spot Nessie

☐ ☐ ☐ pose for Brandon Stanton of *Humans of New York* fame

☐ ☐ ☐ sail on a catamaran, dhow, junk, sloop, and schooner and pick a favourite

☐ ☐ ☐ say "veni, vidi, vici" whenever you walk out of the toilets at work

☐ ☐ ☐ buy an old vardo wagon and turn it into a reading room

☐ ☐ ☐ toast marshmallows in your fireplace

☐ ☐ ☐ get a haircut and donate the clippings to Locks of Love

☐ ☐ ☐ gird your loins and taste testicle terrine in Iceland

☐ ☐ ☐ swim off Martha's Vineyard and try not to think about *Jaws*

☐ ☐ ☐ book a cuddle therapy session

☐ ☐ ☐ infiltrate the Freemasons and see what happens

☐ ☐ ☐ drive by *The Fresh Prince of Bel-Air* house in Brentwood, California

☐ ☐ ☐ campaign the Academy to add "Best Stunts" to the Oscars

☐ ☐ ☐ wear four-foot-long Mexican pointy boots

☐ ☐ ☐ take a pic of the Asahi Golden Turd in Tokyo, Japan

☐ ☐ ☐ go from basic bitch to boss bitch

☐ ☐ ☐ practise *lojong*

☐ ☐ ☐ attend Art Basel in Miami, Florida

☐ ☐ ☐ pray to Saint Bibiana to cure your hangover

☐ ☐ ☐ prepare for end days at the Bear Grylls Survival Academy

☐ ☐ ☐ enter a cheese-rolling competition

☐ ☐ ☐ run for mayor

☐ ☐ ☐ make Goop's Sex Bark and see if it makes you horny

☐ ☐ ☐ play the kazoo

☐ ☐ ☐ explore the colourful Chichicastenango Cemetery in Guatemala

☐ ☐ ☐ come up with fake aphorisms

☐ ☐ ☐ run the Athens Classic
Marathon in Greece

☐ ☐ ☐ play naked Twister

☐ ☐ ☐ host a Friendsgiving

☐ ☐ ☐ experience the long
Minnesota goodbye

☐ ☐ ☐ kiss the Blarney Stone
in Ireland

☐ ☐ ☐ buy an adult-size onesie

☐ ☐ ☐ eat only waffles for a week

☐ ☐ ☐ learn all twenty-seven Albanian words
for "moustache"

☐ ☐ ☐ roast a pig on a spit

☐ ☐ ☐ walk along the Bund in Shanghai, China

☐ ☐ ☐ screen your film at a film festival

☐ ☐ ☐ stand under a waterfall

☐ ☐ ☐ adopt a *zakka* aesthetic

☐ ☐ ☐ edify yourself

☐ ☐ ☐ see a beaver in the wild

☐ ☐ ☐ refuse to part with your old papasan chair

☐ ☐ ☐ win a bake-off with one of your
grandma's recipes

☐ ☐ ☐ spend a day at the Art Institute in
Chicago, Illinois

☐ ☐ ☐ make a Tater Tot casserole

☐ ☐ ☐ stay at the Lizzie Borden B&B in
Fall River, Massachusetts

☐ ☐ ☐ volunteer at a polling station

☐ ☐ ☐ visit Monet's Garden in Giverny, France

☐ ☐ ☐ take as many pics of your second child as you
did of your first

☐ ☐ ☐ go fly-fishing

☐ ☐ ☐ have your tea leaves read

☐ ☐ ☐ decide what you would want on your backstage rider even if you aren't in a band

☐ ☐ ☐ buy a jukebox

☐ ☐ ☐ grind fresh coffee beans every morning

☐ ☐ ☐ fully commit and dunk yourself at a polar bear swim

☐ ☐ ☐ climb the Staircase to Heaven in Oahu, Hawaii

☐ ☐ ☐ sit in the stands for a FIFA World Cup match

☐ ☐ ☐ be afraid and do it anyway

☐ ☐ ☐ consult a naturopathic doctor

☐ ☐ ☐ watch a sumo tournament

☐ ☐ ☐ visit the Citadelle la Ferrière in Haiti

☐ ☐ ☐ stay up for seventy-two hours straight – just to see if you can

☐ ☐ ☐ meet a never-nude

☐ ☐ ☐ read all of Anaïs Nin's books

☐ ☐ ☐ invent a Richter scale for gassiness

☐ ☐ ☐ ride the Duquesne Incline funicular in Pittsburgh, Pennsylvania

☐ ☐ ☐ drink bhang lassi

☐ ☐ ☐ meet Petros the Pelican III on Mykonos, Greece

☐ ☐ ☐ suck on someone's toes

☐ ☐ ☐ teach yourself to be ambidextrous

☐ ☐ ☐ put on a red swimsuit and run down the beach *Baywatch*-style

☐ ☐ ☐ learn what a schmuck really is

☐ ☐ ☐ stay at the Fairmont Le Château Frontenac in Quebec, Canada

☐ ☐ ☐ collect sock monkeys

☐ ☐ ☐ crack an egg with a triple yolk

☐ ☐ ☐ party at Oktoberfest in Germany

☐ ☐ ☐ use opera glasses instead of binoculars

☐ ☐ ☐ see a play in London's West End

☐ ☐ ☐ ride on a parade float

☐ ☐ ☐ practise selective hearing around those spewing negativity

☐ ☐ ☐ adopt a gerbil and name him Richard Gere

☐ ☐ ☐ go inside the Blue Grotto in Capri, Italy

☐ ☐ ☐ drink a Sazerac in New Orleans, Louisiana

☐ ☐ ☐ find an occasion to wear a gown other than a wedding or prom

☐ ☐ ☐ ditch your digital camera for a Polaroid

☐ ☐ ☐ celebrate Julefrokost

☐ ☐ ☐ get a patent for an invention

☐ ☐ ☐ visit the Center for Disease Control Museum in Atlanta, Georgia

☐ ☐ ☐ take some echinacea before you go

☐ ☐ ☐ bowl a perfect game

☐ ☐ ☐ climb up a water tower

☐ ☐ ☐ stop biting your nails

☐ ☐ ☐ watch all of Richard Linklater's movies

☐ ☐ ☐ ride a tandem bike

☐ ☐ ☐ live in a drinking town with a fishing problem

☐ ☐ ☐ survey your girlfriends and see if the
McClintock effect is in effect

☐ ☐ ☐ admire the painted village of Zalipie in Poland

☐ ☐ ☐ petition to have pumpkin spice added to the
UNESCO Intangible Cultural Heritage List

☐ ☐ ☐ meet a flat-earther and pat them gently on
the head

☐ ☐ ☐ sit inside one of the Watts Towers in
Los Angeles, California

☐ ☐ ☐ play the bodhran

☐ ☐ ☐ learn to swallow a sword

☐ ☐ ☐ dress up your kid
as your mini-me

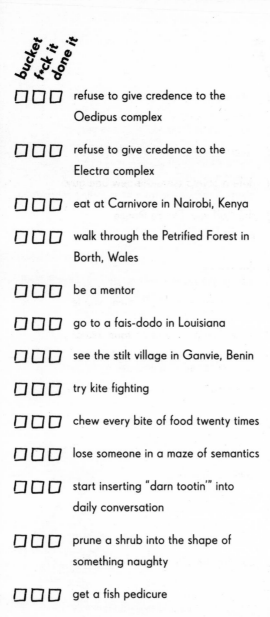

bucket / f*ck it / done it

☐ ☐ ☐ refuse to give credence to the Oedipus complex

☐ ☐ ☐ refuse to give credence to the Electra complex

☐ ☐ ☐ eat at Carnivore in Nairobi, Kenya

☐ ☐ ☐ walk through the Petrified Forest in Borth, Wales

☐ ☐ ☐ be a mentor

☐ ☐ ☐ go to a fais-dodo in Louisiana

☐ ☐ ☐ see the stilt village in Ganvie, Benin

☐ ☐ ☐ try kite fighting

☐ ☐ ☐ chew every bite of food twenty times

☐ ☐ ☐ lose someone in a maze of semantics

☐ ☐ ☐ start inserting "darn tootin'" into daily conversation

☐ ☐ ☐ prune a shrub into the shape of something naughty

☐ ☐ ☐ get a fish pedicure

☐ ☐ ☐ take a pic of the Hundertwasserhaus in
Vienna, Austria

☐ ☐ ☐ cleverly conceal your Achilles' heel

☐ ☐ ☐ date a SNAG (sensitive new age guy)

☐ ☐ ☐ show off your Dance Dance
Revolution skills

☐ ☐ ☐ throw a rager

☐ ☐ ☐ call someone out for throwing shade

☐ ☐ ☐ force a misogynist to perform one of
The Vagina Monologues publicly

☐ ☐ ☐ make macaroni with ten kinds of cheese

☐ ☐ ☐ join a beach clean

☐ ☐ ☐ slide down the natural Waitava Waterslide
in Fiji

☐ ☐ ☐ memorise the capitals of all the countries in
the world

☐ ☐ ☐ buy Maison Gatti chairs for your patio

☐ ☐ ☐ bungee jump

☐ ☐ ☐ sail safely through the Graveyard of the Great Lakes

☐ ☐ ☐ stroll the length of Sydney's Great Coastal Walk in Australia

☐ ☐ ☐ explore the Alhambra in Granada, Spain

☐ ☐ ☐ swap your flip-flops for Japanese geta

☐ ☐ ☐ try synchronised swimming

☐ ☐ ☐ wow someone with the factoid that a banana is actually a giant herb

☐ ☐ ☐ adopt a raw food diet

☐ ☐ ☐ watch a glacier calve

☐ ☐ ☐ eat Solomon Gundy

☐ ☐ ☐ eat salmagundi

☐ ☐ ☐ leave an ex-voto at a shrine

☐ ☐ ☐ hang glide

☐ ☐ ☐ join a zombie walk

☐ ☐ ☐ spot a pink dolphin in the Amazon

bucket
f*ck it
done it

☐☐☐ create an illusory contour

☐☐☐ keep a list of every movie you've ever watched

☐☐☐ pray for a Talking Heads reunion at the
Sanctuary of Our Lady of Lourdes in France

☐☐☐ visit the village of Climax in Saskatchewan,
Canada

☐☐☐ check out the "Come Again Soon" sign on the
way out of town

☐☐☐ keep a list of every book you've ever read

EVERY MOVIE I HAVE SEEN:

1. HARRY POTTER + THE PHILOSOPHER'S STONE.
2. HARRY POTTER + THE CHAMBER OF SECRETS.
3. HARRY POTTER + THE PRISONER OF AZKABAN.
4. HARRY POTTER + THE GOBLET OF FIRE.
5. HARRY POTTER + THE ORDER OF THE PHOENIX.
6. HARRY POTTER + THE HALF BLOOD PRINCE.
7. HARRY POTTER + THE DEATHLY HALLOWS P.1
8. HARRY POTTER + THE DEATHLY HALLOWS P.2

EVERY BOOK I HAVE READ:

1. HARRY POTTER + THE PHILOSOPHER'S STONE.
2. HARRY POTTER + THE CHAMBER OF SECRETS.
3. HARRY POTTER + THE PRISONER OF AZKABAN.
4. HARRY POTTER + GOBLET OF FIRE.
5. HARRY POTTER + THE ORDER OF THE PHOENIX.
6. HARRY POTTER + THE HALF BLOOD PRINCE.
7. HARRY POTTER + THE DEATHLY HALLOWS.

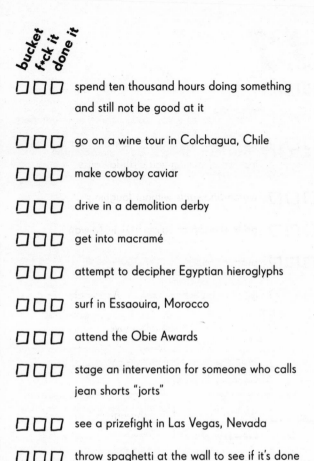

bucket
f*ck it
done it

☐ ☐ ☐ spend ten thousand hours doing something and still not be good at it

☐ ☐ ☐ go on a wine tour in Colchagua, Chile

☐ ☐ ☐ make cowboy caviar

☐ ☐ ☐ drive in a demolition derby

☐ ☐ ☐ get into macramé

☐ ☐ ☐ attempt to decipher Egyptian hieroglyphs

☐ ☐ ☐ surf in Essaouira, Morocco

☐ ☐ ☐ attend the Obie Awards

☐ ☐ ☐ stage an intervention for someone who calls jean shorts "jorts"

☐ ☐ ☐ see a prizefight in Las Vegas, Nevada

☐ ☐ ☐ throw spaghetti at the wall to see if it's done

☐ ☐ ☐ ride a horse using a sidesaddle

☐ ☐ ☐ call a spade a spade

☐ ☐ ☐ eat cake at Versailles in France

☐ ☐ ☐ paint a triptych

☐ ☐ ☐ use Mendel's laws to guess what colour eyes your baby will have

☐ ☐ ☐ ask friends and family to donate to a charity instead of buying you birthday gifts

☐ ☐ ☐ watch *Showgirls* without laughing

☐ ☐ ☐ go to the top of Taipei 101 in Taiwan

☐ ☐ ☐ practice *huna*

☐ ☐ ☐ listen to bluegrass music in Appalachia

☐ ☐ ☐ observe a sloth actually move

☐ ☐ ☐ programme the voice inside your head to sound like Viola Davis's

☐ ☐ ☐ drive a Pontiac Aztec through Albuquerque, New Mexico

☐ ☐ ☐ enjoy fifteen minutes of fame

NEWS
LOCAL WOMAN SURVIVES FRUIT FLY ATTACK

☐ ☐ ☐ compose a concerto

☐ ☐ ☐ eat lumpy dick

☐ ☐ ☐ eat spotted dick

☐ ☐ ☐ play badminton

☐ ☐ ☐ hate the player and hate the game

☐ ☐ ☐ ride in a Riva Aquarama on Lake Como in Italy

☐ ☐ ☐ balance your chi

☐ ☐ ☐ colour with every crayon in the box

☐ ☐ ☐ notice that Wenceslas Square in Prague is actually more of a rectangle

☐ ☐ ☐ forgive someone who doesn't deserve it

☐ ☐ ☐ ring the opening bell at the NYSE

☐ ☐ ☐ go on a blind date set up by a person, not an app

☐ ☐ ☐ use an hourglass instead of a timer

☐ ☐ ☐ visit Dinosaur Provincial Park in Alberta, Canada

☐ ☐ ☐ create a meme

☐ ☐ ☐ have your meme go viral

☐ ☐ ☐ summit Denali in Alaska

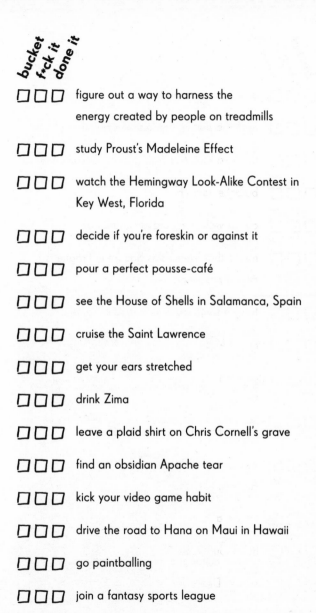

□	□	□	figure out a way to harness the energy created by people on treadmills
□	□	□	study Proust's Madeleine Effect
□	□	□	watch the Hemingway Look-Alike Contest in Key West, Florida
□	□	□	decide if you're foreskin or against it
□	□	□	pour a perfect pousse-café
□	□	□	see the House of Shells in Salamanca, Spain
□	□	□	cruise the Saint Lawrence
□	□	□	get your ears stretched
□	□	□	drink Zima
□	□	□	leave a plaid shirt on Chris Cornell's grave
□	□	□	find an obsidian Apache tear
□	□	□	kick your video game habit
□	□	□	drive the road to Hana on Maui in Hawaii
□	□	□	go paintballing
□	□	□	join a fantasy sports league

bucket f*ck it done it

☐ ☐ ☐ gather your cojones and eat *shirako* in Japan

☐ ☐ ☐ watch a ship go through the Miraflores Locks at the Panama Canal

☐ ☐ ☐ spice a recipe with *dukkah*

☐ ☐ ☐ lower a portcullis

☐ ☐ ☐ celebrate Tet in Vietnam

☐ ☐ ☐ attend a soirée

☐ ☐ ☐ retry a food you hate because the average life span of a taste bud is ten days

☐ ☐ ☐ take an avalanche safety course

☐ ☐ ☐ suck the brains out of a prawn

☐ ☐ ☐ go to a show at the Troubadour in Hollywood, California

☐ ☐ ☐ find out if the carpet matches the drapes

☐ ☐ ☐ drink champagne through a crazy straw

☐ ☐ ☐ visit the blue city of Jodhpur, India

☐ ☐ ☐ see the goats on the roof of the Old Country Market in Coombs, Canada

☐ ☐ ☐ choose your DJ name, even if you'll never be one

☐ ☐ ☐ scour estate sales for undiscovered treasures

☐ ☐ ☐ watch an Aussie Rules Football game

☐ ☐ ☐ refuse to date someone whose text bubbles are green

☐ ☐ ☐ explore Acadia National Forest in Maine

☐ ☐ ☐ drink a mai tai at Trader Vic's

☐ ☐ ☐ ask a German if *backpfeifengesicht* really means "a face in need of a fist"

☐ ☐ ☐ go paragliding

☐ ☐ ☐ salsa

☐ ☐ ☐ enrol in clown school

☐ ☐ ☐ set boundaries with your cat

☐ ☐ ☐ eat at Antica Pizzeria Port'Alba – the world's oldest pizzeria – in Naples, Italy

☐ ☐ ☐ meet someone with no filter

☐ ☐ ☐ get your teeth whitened

☐ ☐ ☐ draw fashion inspiration from Helena Bonham Carter

☐ ☐ ☐ swing on the Swing at the End of the World in Banos, Ecuador

☐ ☐ ☐ follow the teachings of the Dude

☐ ☐ ☐ try all sixteen hundred Belgian beers

☐ ☐ ☐ go bombing with a graffiti artist

☐ ☐ ☐ heed Confucius and "dig two graves before you embark on a journey of revenge"

☐ ☐ ☐ wear crotchless underwear

☐ ☐ ☐ join the November Project stair climb at Harvard Stadium in Boston, Massachusetts

☐ ☐ ☐ show someone your moles in the name of maculomancy

☐ ☐ ☐ buy a Marcel Breuer Wassily chair

☐ ☐ ☐ study Catalan modernism

☐ ☐ ☐ luge

☐ ☐ ☐ decorate with rosemaling pieces

☐ ☐ ☐ catch a blue lobster

☐ ☐ ☐ explore Tiger Cave in Belize

☐ ☐ ☐ attend the Olympics

☐ ☐ ☐ attend the Paralympics

☐ ☐ ☐ attend the Special Olympics

☐ ☐ ☐ visit Flannery O'Connor's childhood home in Savannah, Georgia

☐ ☐ ☐ buy your clothing used to lessen your impact on the environment

☐ ☐ ☐ stuff your face at a buffet, trash panda-style

☐ ☐ ☐ go tramping in New Zealand

☐ ☐ ☐ learn to speak Mandarin

☐ ☐ ☐ stay in an over-water bungalow in Bora-Bora, Tahiti

☐ ☐ ☐ drive a Tesla

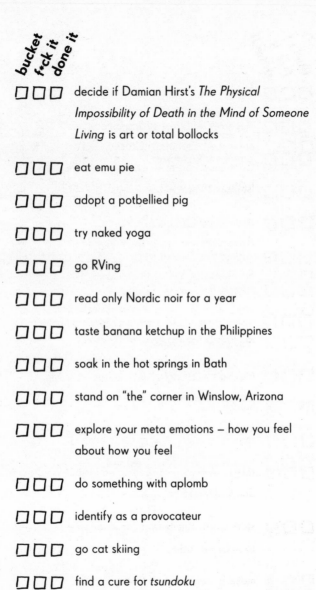

bucket
f*ck it
done it

☐ ☐ ☐ decide if Damian Hirst's *The Physical Impossibility of Death in the Mind of Someone Living* is art or total bollocks

☐ ☐ ☐ eat emu pie

☐ ☐ ☐ adopt a potbellied pig

☐ ☐ ☐ try naked yoga

☐ ☐ ☐ go RVing

☐ ☐ ☐ read only Nordic noir for a year

☐ ☐ ☐ taste banana ketchup in the Philippines

☐ ☐ ☐ soak in the hot springs in Bath

☐ ☐ ☐ stand on "the" corner in Winslow, Arizona

☐ ☐ ☐ explore your meta emotions – how you feel about how you feel

☐ ☐ ☐ do something with aplomb

☐ ☐ ☐ identify as a provocateur

☐ ☐ ☐ go cat skiing

☐ ☐ ☐ find a cure for *tsundoku*

☐ ☐ ☐ pay a street artist to draw your caricature

☐ ☐ ☐ enter the Bosphorous Cross Continental Swim in Istanbul, Turkey

☐ ☐ ☐ secretly subscribe to *Il Mio Papa* pope magazine for someone

☐ ☐ ☐ drink Crème Yvette violet liqueur

☐ ☐ ☐ carry a tin of Parma Violets in your bag

☐ ☐ ☐ drive the NC500 Loop in Scotland

☐ ☐ ☐ resist the urge to get a tattoo

☐ ☐ ☐ humblebrag

☐ ☐ ☐ regrow a celery stalk from its base

☐ ☐ ☐ take a workshop at the Esalen Institute in Big Sur, California

☐ ☐ ☐ start a new family tradition and force everyone to take part

☐ ☐ ☐ make a hoecake

☐ ☐ ☐   get a thalassotherapy treatment at a spa

☐ ☐ ☐   eat gnocchi on Day of the Gnocchi
in Argentina

☐ ☐ ☐   see a Monkey Face orchid

☐ ☐ ☐   use Marseille soap

☐ ☐ ☐   practise mindfulness meditation

☐ ☐ ☐   learn to say "faster, faster, don't stop" in five
different languages

☐ ☐ ☐   ride a double-decker bus

☐ ☐ ☐   quote Susan Sontag

☐ ☐ ☐   infiltrate Club 33 at Disneyland and see
what happens

☐ ☐ ☐   meet an impresario

☐ ☐ ☐   cheer for anyone except the
New York Yankees

☐ ☐ ☐   swim straight after eating

☐ ☐ ☐   attend the Design Indaba Conference in
Cape Town, South Africa

bucket	f*ck it	done it

☐ ☐ ☐ organise a flyting – a Viking-style roast battle

☐ ☐ ☐ go on a vision quest

☐ ☐ ☐ take up taxidermy

☐ ☐ ☐ compete in the World Taxidermy and Fish Carving Championships

☐ ☐ ☐ chill with a Hawaiian shave ice

☐ ☐ ☐ give anyone who says "I only like their earlier work" a slow clap

☐ ☐ ☐ stand outside *The Today Show* with a sign (if you must)

☐ ☐ ☐ see the world's biggest wine collection in Milestii Mici, Moldova

☐ ☐ ☐ worship all things maple syrup at a sugar shack in Quebec, Canada

☐ ☐ ☐ peel an orange so the peel looks like an elephant

☐ ☐ ☐ ride in a gondola in Venice, Italy

☐ ☐ ☐ ride in a gondola at the Venetian in Las Vegas, Nevada

☐ ☐ ☐ get high and look at Hieronymus Bosch's artwork

☐ ☐ ☐ drink Dr Brown's Cel-Ray soda

☐ ☐ ☐ deep dive into a Wikipedia rabbit hole and surface hours later none the smarter

☐ ☐ ☐ eat a pork butt sandwich

☐ ☐ ☐ eat *halo-halo*

☐ ☐ ☐ see a beaver moon

☐ ☐ ☐ make chowchow

☐ ☐ ☐ make piccalilli

☐ ☐ ☐ skip school and watch *Ferris Bueller's Day Off*

☐ ☐ ☐ go to a Rodgers and Hammerstein musical

☐ ☐ ☐ walk through the Red Light District in Amsterdam, Netherlands

☐ ☐ ☐ stand on the corner of Clinton Drive and Fidelity Street in Houston, Texas

☐ ☐ ☐ be immune to hat head

☐ ☐ ☐ buy a Scandinavian kitchen witch for luck

☐ ☐ ☐ visit all of Le Corbusier's buildings

☐ ☐ ☐ sing in a choir

☐ ☐ ☐ aerobicise to Richard Simmons's *Sweatin' to the Oldies*

☐ ☐ ☐ stay at Palacio del Sal in Bolivia – a hotel made of salt

☐ ☐ ☐ learn the difference between a blazer, sport coat, and suit jacket

☐ ☐ ☐ look dope in all three jackets

☐ ☐ ☐ visit Poopoo Land poop museum in South Korea

☐ ☐ ☐ confiscate someone's scrunchies

☐ ☐ ☐ start saying "it's on like ping-pong" every time before you serve

☐ ☐ ☐ see a pangolin in the wild

☐ ☐ ☐ be a thank-you-note-sending kind of person

☐ ☐ ☐ drive through Monument Valley in Arizona

☐ ☐ ☐ describe yourself as a bon vivant

☐ ☐ ☐ check the Vegas odds on your team winning the Stanley Cup

☐ ☐ ☐ memorise all the words to every song in *Mamma Mia*

☐ ☐ ☐ sink your teeth into competitive eating

☐ ☐ ☐ make floam

☐ ☐ ☐ fan dance

☐ ☐ ☐ learn to love okra

☐ ☐ ☐ fish for your dinner at Zauo Shinjuku restaurant in Tokyo, Japan

☐ ☐ ☐ cleverly disguise your underboob sweat

☐ ☐ ☐ embrace your introverted nature

☐ ☐ ☐ embrace your ambiverted nature

☐ ☐ ☐ embrace your extroverted nature

☐ ☐ ☐ give yellow Starbursts some love, too

☐ ☐ ☐ go up the Eiffel Tower in
Paris, France

☐ ☐ ☐ meet a *raggare* in Sweden

☐ ☐ ☐ eat at a *kafe*, *restoran*,
kofeynya, *pab*, *stolovaya*, and *zakusochnaya*
in Russia

☐ ☐ ☐ strip off on a nude beach

☐ ☐ ☐ admit that you hate craft beer in a hipster bar

☐ ☐ ☐ make a marigold garland

☐ ☐ ☐ create a Pavlovian response in your partner
where they hear a song and suddenly want to
rub your feet

☐ ☐ ☐ find a cure for seasonal affective disorder

☐ ☐ ☐ convince someone that they're right- or left-
brained based on the hand they write with

☐ ☐ ☐ paddleboard

☐ ☐ ☐ use an abacus

☐ ☐ ☐ visit the Icelandic Elf School in
Reykjavík, Iceland

bucket
f*ck it
done it

☐ ☐ ☐ go to a David Choe exhibit

☐ ☐ ☐ line dance

☐ ☐ ☐ bring your bike to the Blessing of the Bicycles
at the Cathedral of Saint John the Divine in
New York, New York

☐ ☐ ☐ get a genital piercing

☐ ☐ ☐ try haggis hurling (that's throwing, not puking)

☐ ☐ ☐ see a naturally occurring whirlpool

☐ ☐ ☐ hike the length of the West Coast Trail

☐ ☐ ☐ sport a hi-top fade

☐ ☐ ☐ enter the Henley-on-Todd Regatta in
Alice Springs, Australia – the world's only dry
river race

☐ ☐ ☐ apprentice as a milliner

☐ ☐ ☐ go to circus school

☐ ☐ ☐ eat a Philly cheesesteak in Philadelphia,
Pennsylvania

☐ ☐ ☐ play beach tennis

☐ ☐ ☐ hear proof that you're not the only one trying not to fart in yoga

☐ ☐ ☐ see the elephant seals outside San Simeon, California

☐ ☐ ☐ embrace an au natural look and stop wearing makeup

☐ ☐ ☐ compete in a snocross event

☐ ☐ ☐ drink rosé all day

☐ ☐ ☐ melt down old jewellery and have something new made

☐ ☐ ☐ drink chestnut beer in Corsica, France

☐ ☐ ☐ visit Point Barrow, Alaska – the northernmost point in the United States

☐ ☐ ☐ visit Ka Lae, Hawaii – the southernmost point in the United States

☐ ☐ ☐ visit West Quoddy Head, Maine – the easternmost point in the United States

☐ ☐ ☐ visit Cape Wrangell, Alaska – the westernmost point in the United States

bucket	f*ck it	done it	
☐	☐	☐	pose nude for an art class
☐	☐	☐	buy a *krama* scarf in Cambodia
☐	☐	☐	get into cosplay
☐	☐	☐	make your own bitters
☐	☐	☐	inflate 99 red balloons
☐	☐	☐	watch all of the movies that have won an Oscar for Best Picture since 1929
☐	☐	☐	study ontology
☐	☐	☐	snuggle-fuck to stay warm during a polar vortex
☐	☐	☐	go microwave-free
☐	☐	☐	go on holiday without taking a single picture
☐	☐	☐	be known for a signature hot dish
☐	☐	☐	try quilling
☐	☐	☐	give tough love when it's warranted
☐	☐	☐	see a herd of paparazzi

☐ ☐ ☐ make a reservation at the Imperial Hotel in Tokyo under the name Bob Harris

☐ ☐ ☐ check your privilege

☐ ☐ ☐ swear off emojis for a week

☐ ☐ ☐ walk around the Signpost Forest in Watson Lake, Canada

☐ ☐ ☐ watch a streetball game at the Cage in New York, New York

☐ ☐ ☐ listen to rock operas

☐ ☐ ☐ take someone's thumb ring and put it in a safe place where no one will find it ever again

☐ ☐ ☐ boulder in Fontainebleau, France

☐ ☐ ☐ reenact Monty Python silly walks in public

☐ ☐ ☐ make an anatomically correct scarecrow

☐ ☐ ☐ programme the voice inside your head to sound like Morgan Freeman

☐ ☐ ☐ identify as a jezebel

☐ ☐ ☐ drive a donk

bucket
f*ck it
done it

☐ ☐ ☐ visit Author's Ridge at the Sleepy Hollow
Cemetery in Concord, Massachusetts

☐ ☐ ☐ look up at a *moko jumbie*

☐ ☐ ☐ drink sugarcane juice

☐ ☐ ☐ explore the Gardens by the Bay in Singapore

☐ ☐ ☐ people-watch on the boardwalk in Atlantic
City, New Jersey

☐ ☐ ☐ practise lateral thinking

☐ ☐ ☐ run the Tromso Midnight Sun Marathon
in Norway

☐ ☐ ☐ attend the Taurus World Stunt Awards

☐ ☐ ☐ eat corn on the cob without needing to
floss right after

☐ ☐ ☐ rescue someone from a sharting   incident

☐ ☐ ☐ search for alien life in
Roswell, New Mexico,
and Varginha, Brazil

bucket
f*ck it
done it

☐ ☐ ☐ take singing lessons

☐ ☐ ☐ meet a Hungarian cowboy

☐ ☐ ☐ sign with an agent

☐ ☐ ☐ play kubb

☐ ☐ ☐ wash your hair with
beer and keep your mouth open

☐ ☐ ☐ watch Mexican jumping beans jump

☐ ☐ ☐ surf the manmade Eisbach River in
Munich, Germany

☐ ☐ ☐ wear a black diamond ring

☐ ☐ ☐ never be the nerd who asks for a trick instead
of just giving out a treat

☐ ☐ ☐ have a pocket square for every occasion

☐ ☐ ☐ dye your hair lilac

☐ ☐ ☐ visit the Museum of Bad Art in
Somerville, Massachusetts

☐ ☐ ☐ list all of Batman's villains from the comics,
shows, and movies

☐ ☐ ☐ visit the sister cities of Boring, Oregon, and Dull, Scotland

☐ ☐ ☐ date a sapiosexual

☐ ☐ ☐ carry a sceptre around and see what happens

☐ ☐ ☐ humour your inner hippy and tie-dye something

☐ ☐ ☐ get caught on the kiss cam at an American football game

☐ ☐ ☐ drink coconut water and not get all holier than thou

☐ ☐ ☐ see the *Jeanneke Pis*, *Manneken Pis*, and *Het Zinneke* sculptures in Brussels, Belgium

☐ ☐ ☐ say "pad kid poured curd pulled cod" – the world's hardest tongue twister – three times fast

☐ ☐ ☐ go mushroom hunting

☐ ☐ ☐ eat crackling

☐ ☐ ☐ wear a jumpsuit, but don't drink anything so you don't have to strip down in a public toilet

☐ ☐ ☐ stay at Amangiri in Canyon Point, Utah

☐ ☐ ☐ stargaze

☐ ☐ ☐ do the CN Tower EdgeWalk in
Toronto, Canada

☐ ☐ ☐ try oil pulling

☐ ☐ ☐ buy a Daruma doll for luck

☐ ☐ ☐ attend the El Colacho baby-jumping festival in
Castrillo de Murcia, Spain

☐ ☐ ☐ give your date a Christian
side hug

☐ ☐ ☐ use a yoni egg

☐ ☐ ☐ write a play

☐ ☐ ☐ ask your mother what she craved
while pregnant and see if it's your
favourite food

☐ ☐ ☐ visit the Italianate village of Portmeirion
in Wales

☐ ☐ ☐ make a woodblock print

☐ ☐ ☐ co-parent a pet after a successful conscious uncoupling

☐ ☐ ☐ play polo

☐ ☐ ☐ stroll along the Riva in Split, Croatia

☐ ☐ ☐ win a tug-of-war

☐ ☐ ☐ wear mukluks

☐ ☐ ☐ call LaCroix what it is – the Emperor's New Clothes of beverages

☐ ☐ ☐ see a Fabergé egg

☐ ☐ ☐ have a May/December romance

☐ ☐ ☐ eat colourful *kek lapis* cake in Sarawak, Indonesia

☐ ☐ ☐ compete in the Ironman

☐ ☐ ☐ practise Holotropic Breathwork

☐ ☐ ☐ hire a majordomo

☐ ☐ ☐ read all of 50 Cent's G-Unit books

☐ ☐ ☐ meet Jonathan the tortoise in Saint Helena

☐ ☐ ☐ become a bone broth devotee

☐ ☐ ☐ celebrate Samhain

☐ ☐ ☐ identify as a cat lady

☐ ☐ ☐ dodge a cow on
the street in India

☐ ☐ ☐ decide if you would
rather fight a horse-size
duck or a hundred duck-size horses

☐ ☐ ☐ drive the length of Route 66 in the
United States

☐ ☐ ☐ stop at all of the roadside attractions
along the way

☐ ☐ ☐ do everything in your power to never wear
business casual

☐ ☐ ☐ gather your cojones and eat *andouillette*
in France

☐ ☐ ☐ see the Rockettes perform

☐ ☐ ☐ learn the difference between port
and starboard

☐ ☐ ☐ manage to sleep on an aeroplane

☐ ☐ ☐ visit the David Hasselhoff Museum in Berlin, Germany

☐ ☐ ☐ choose to properly spell and punctuate all of your texts

☐ ☐ ☐ use rose water instead of perfume

☐ ☐ ☐ participate in an Outward Bound expedition

☐ ☐ ☐ listen to Tommy Cash's song "I Didn't Walk the Line"

☐ ☐ ☐ adopt a pet bunny and name it Alex Forrest

☐ ☐ ☐ enter your bunny in rabbit agility competitions

☐ ☐ ☐ eat *kokoda* in Fiji

☐ ☐ ☐ work as a voice actor

☐ ☐ ☐ order a drink from the Starbucks Secret Menu

☐ ☐ ☐ stay at the whimsical Inntel Hotel in Zaandam, Netherlands

☐ ☐ ☐ show some sideboob

☐ ☐ ☐ prove that the Illuminati exists

☐ ☐ ☐ get a CBD massage

☐ ☐ ☐ fill your pockets with breath mints and head to the Gilroy Garlic Festival in California

☐ ☐ ☐ try a bee venom apitherapy treatment

☐ ☐ ☐ watch *wuxia* movies

☐ ☐ ☐ trek to Vinicunca Rainbow Mountain in Peru

☐ ☐ ☐ wake and bake

☐ ☐ ☐ take ayahuasca with a shaman

☐ ☐ ☐ go deep-sea fishing

☐ ☐ ☐ attend Seoul Fashion Week in South Korea

☐ ☐ ☐ attend Melbourne Fashion Week in Australia

☐ ☐ ☐ attend Tel Aviv Fashion Week in Israel

☐ ☐ ☐ play a duet on the piano

☐ ☐ ☐ have a conversation using only rhyming couplets

☐ ☐ ☐ stay in touch with all of your cousins

☐ ☐ ☐ attend the Piolet d'Or Awards

☐ ☐ ☐ shop at the Galleria Vittorio Emanuele II in Milan, Italy

☐ ☐ ☐ drink a mojito in Cuba

☐ ☐ ☐ sport victory rolls

☐ ☐ ☐ frame all of your accomplishments, even your credit score

☐ ☐ ☐ consult a pet psychic

☐ ☐ ☐ get your picture on the Wheaties box

☐ ☐ ☐ freeze your eggs

☐ ☐ ☐ island-hop in the Galapagos

☐ ☐ ☐ wear a muumuu

☐ ☐ ☐ Nae Nae

☐ ☐ ☐ order a dessert with edible gold leaf on it

bucket
f*ck it
done it

☐ ☐ ☐ stay at the Versace Mansion (Villa Casa Casuarina) in Miami, Florida

☐ ☐ ☐ take up aircraft spotting

☐ ☐ ☐ ask a question before you go to sleep and find the answer in your dreams

☐ ☐ ☐ save up £10,000 to buy the 24-carat gold-plated Inez dildo

☐ ☐ ☐ cruise the Ganges

☐ ☐ ☐ attend the Jane Austen Festival in Bath

☐ ☐ ☐ set up an aquaponics system in your garden

☐ ☐ ☐ write on paper made of elephant dung

☐ ☐ ☐ visit the Hockey Hall of Fame in Toronto, Canada

☐ ☐ ☐ eat soup dumplings

☐ ☐ ☐ provide something borrowed or something blue

☐ ☐ ☐ find out why your dog's paws smell like popcorn

bucket	f*ck it	done it	
☐	☐	☐	see El Árbol del Tule – the world's girthiest tree – in Oaxaca, Mexico
☐	☐	☐	pick a secret word à la Pee-wee Herman, and scream whenever you hear it
☐	☐	☐	watch all of Spike Jonze's music videos
☐	☐	☐	wear a merkin
☐	☐	☐	cruise west on Mulholland Drive at sunset
☐	☐	☐	brown bag it for a month and use the money saved for a next-level dinner out
☐	☐	☐	install a Tin Lizzie horn in your car
☐	☐	☐	see a business of ferrets

☐ ☐ ☐ buy kente cloth in Ghana

☐ ☐ ☐ go to a David Hockney exhibit

☐ ☐ ☐ catch sight of a will-o'-the-wisp in a swamp

☐ ☐ ☐ wash your laundry with soap nuts instead
of detergent

☐ ☐ ☐ raft the Tara River in Montenegro

☐ ☐ ☐ listen to a hip hopera

☐ ☐ ☐ see Misty Copeland dance

☐ ☐ ☐ flyboard

☐ ☐ ☐ ask a stranger to pull your finger

☐ ☐ ☐ feel all of the feels

☐ ☐ ☐ breakfast at Tiffany's the Blue Box Café in
New York, New York

☐ ☐ ☐ celebrate Goonies Day in Astoria, Oregon

☐ ☐ ☐ collect vintage *Playboy* magazines

☐ ☐ ☐ float in the Dead Sea

☐ ☐ ☐ identify as a grammarian

bucket f*ck it done it

☐ ☐ ☐ eat Cheetos with a spoon to avoid
orange fingers

☐ ☐ ☐ describe something as Byzantine

☐ ☐ ☐ party at Nikki Beach in Saint Barth's

☐ ☐ ☐ try underwater rock running

☐ ☐ ☐ sense who will win the Showcase Showdown
on *The Price Is Right* – every time

☐ ☐ ☐ convince someone that the butterfly effect is
when you go from ugly to beautiful

☐ ☐ ☐ learn all forty-seven Hawaiian words
for "banana"

☐ ☐ ☐ hike the length of the Appalachian Trail

☐ ☐ ☐ learn to count cards

☐ ☐ ☐ watch UFC (if you must)

☐ ☐ ☐ refuse to be influenced by an influencer

☐ ☐ ☐ go to the Minnesota State Fair

☐ ☐ ☐ eat Brussels and Liege waffles and pick
a favourite

☐ ☐ ☐ use Kangoo Jumps in public

☐ ☐ ☐ apprentice as a cobbler

☐ ☐ ☐ burn palo santo

☐ ☐ ☐ go on a wine tour in Rioja, Spain

☐ ☐ ☐ draw fashion inspiration from Jane Birkin

☐ ☐ ☐ walk through the Wisteria Tunnel in Kitakyushu, Japan

☐ ☐ ☐ call someone a "slugabed"

☐ ☐ ☐ see *The Thinker* at the Rodin Museum in Paris, France

☐ ☐ ☐ add chia to your diet

☐ ☐ ☐ find a cure for Cotard's syndrome

☐ ☐ ☐ dress up as your favourite meme for Halloween

☐ ☐ ☐ do back handsprings across a gymnasium

☐ ☐ ☐ become a travel hacker

☐ ☐ ☐ swipe right on everyone for a day and see what happens

☐ ☐ ☐ learn to speak Arabic

☐ ☐ ☐ remind someone that if
Britney Spears can get
through 2007, then they can
get through anything

☐ ☐ ☐ stay at the Kennedy School
Hotel in Portland, Oregon,
and sleep in one of the
old classrooms

☐ ☐ ☐ go inside a pharaoh's tomb

☐ ☐ ☐ cook farro for dinner

☐ ☐ ☐ drink fermented mare's milk
in Mongolia

☐ ☐ ☐ explore the ancient city of Bagan in Myanmar

☐ ☐ ☐ have all things in moderation, especially
moderation

☐ ☐ ☐ eat chicken feet at dim sum

☐ ☐ ☐ ride the high-speed Deutsche Bahn
in Germany

☐ ☐ ☐ celebrate the summer solstice

☐ ☐ ☐ celebrate the winter solstice

☐ ☐ ☐ drop a Mars Bar into a public pool

☐ ☐ ☐ give yourself a pump-up speech before your Zumba class

☐ ☐ ☐ buy the *Cookin' with Coolio* cookbook

☐ ☐ ☐ enter the Dakar Rally

☐ ☐ ☐ look through the world's largest kaleidoscope in Mount Tremper, New York

☐ ☐ ☐ weave a tapestry

☐ ☐ ☐ go to a David LaChapelle exhibit

☐ ☐ ☐ try and eat a sumo wrestler's diet for a day

☐ ☐ ☐ tour the MONA Museum in Hobart, Australia

☐ ☐ ☐ do the limbo and see how low you can go

☐ ☐ ☐ prove that you're more than a pretty face

☐ ☐ ☐ drive by Chicken Farmer Rock in Newbury, New Hampshire

bucket	f*ck it	done it	
☐	☐	☐	watch a wiener dog race
☐	☐	☐	drink quinoa vodka and know that is why we can't have nice things
☐	☐	☐	get dirty at Laghetto di Fanghi mud baths in Sicily
☐	☐	☐	take an ikebana class
☐	☐	☐	join a meal delivery service
☐	☐	☐	make your own bath bombs
☐	☐	☐	go rappelling
☐	☐	☐	visit a dominatrix
☐	☐	☐	sail in the Vendée Globe race around the world
☐	☐	☐	ride the Ferris wheel at the top of the Canton Tower in Guangzhou, China
☐	☐	☐	attend the Jazz Age Lawn Party on Governor's Island in New York
☐	☐	☐	see a tapir in the wild
☐	☐	☐	be named poet laureate

☐ ☐ ☐ eat a hushpuppy

☐ ☐ ☐ buy a lebkuchen gingerbread heart

☐ ☐ ☐ wear a *lei po'o*

☐ ☐ ☐ admire the Colosseum in
Rome, Italy

☐ ☐ ☐ practise the
Wim Hof
Method

☐ ☐ ☐ watch all of
John Carpenter's movies

☐ ☐ ☐ ask a German if *brustwarze* (their word for
"nipple") really means "breast wart"

☐ ☐ ☐ call out a catfisher

☐ ☐ ☐ people-watch outside a drive-through wedding
chapel in Las Vegas, Nevada

☐ ☐ ☐ give a manspreader a golf clap

☐ ☐ ☐ settle a dispute by arm wrestling

☐ ☐ ☐ ski the Harakiri run in Mayrhofen, Austria

bucket
f*ck it
done it

☐ ☐ ☐ go on the Meow Meow Cruise – for cat lovers – in the Bahamas

☐ ☐ ☐ try on a coconut bra

☐ ☐ ☐ use beef tallow lip balm

☐ ☐ ☐ fly a drone

☐ ☐ ☐ listen to Britpop

☐ ☐ ☐ take an outdoor shower

☐ ☐ ☐ wear a tutu

☐ ☐ ☐ drink at the Office speakeasy in Chicago, Illinois

☐ ☐ ☐ get your hands on a Pirelli Calendar

☐ ☐ ☐ sport a man bag with confidence

☐ ☐ ☐ buy a Roycroft rocking chair

☐ ☐ ☐ tease your hair and go to a Steel Panther show

☐ ☐ ☐ run the Sparkasse 3-Länder-Marathon through three countries – Austria, Germany, and Switzerland

bucket
f*ck it
done it

☐ ☐ ☐ disregard intentional fallacy when looking at art

☐ ☐ ☐ leave a tube of liquid liner on Amy Winehouse's grave

☐ ☐ ☐ use a Chemex Coffeemaker

☐ ☐ ☐ visit Big Beaver, Pennsylvania

☐ ☐ ☐ collect costume jewellery

☐ ☐ ☐ hike the length of the Kokoda Trail in Papua New Guinea

☐ ☐ ☐ keep a can of squirty cream in your desk and spray some in your mouth when you get hangry

☐ ☐ ☐ add bee pollen to your diet

☐ ☐ ☐ drive a De Tomaso Mangusta

☐ ☐ ☐ eat prosciutto di Parma and *jámon serrano* and pick a favourite

☐ ☐ ☐ try all of the positions in the *Kama Sutra*

☐ ☐ ☐ listen to Mason Bates's *The (R)evolution of Steve Jobs* opera

☐ ☐ ☐ cook with
duck fat

☐ ☐ ☐ swing from
a chandelier

☐ ☐ ☐ attend the
San Sebastián
International Film
Festival in Spain

☐ ☐ ☐ find out if Electronic Voice
Phenomena is truly paranormal

☐ ☐ ☐ enter the International Hair Freezing Contest
at Takhini Hot Pools in Whitehorse, Canada

☐ ☐ ☐ snorkel in Jellyfish Lake in Palau

☐ ☐ ☐ grow your own microgreens

☐ ☐ ☐ drink dandelion wine

☐ ☐ ☐ study cubism

☐ ☐ ☐ go lawn bowling

☐ ☐ ☐ read all of Ursula K. Le Guin's books

☐ ☐ ☐ orchestrate a not-so-hostile takeover

☐ ☐ ☐ meet Jake the Alligator Man at Marsh's Free Museum in Long Beach, Washington

☐ ☐ ☐ get a watercolour tattoo

☐ ☐ ☐ eat a kangaroo burger

☐ ☐ ☐ shotgun a beer

☐ ☐ ☐ ring Tibetan *tingsha* cymbals

☐ ☐ ☐ talk half as much as you listen

☐ ☐ ☐ fangirl over Bill Nye

☐ ☐ ☐ embrace carbs and make a *panzanella* bread salad

☐ ☐ ☐ buy a Louis Vuitton pen

☐ ☐ ☐ buy Gucci wallpaper

☐ ☐ ☐ buy a Chanel basketball

☐ ☐ ☐ stay at the Hang Nga Guesthouse (aka Crazy House) in Dalat, Vietnam

☐ ☐ ☐ see a harvest moon

☐ ☐ ☐ enter your 4x4 in a winch challenge

bucket
f*ck it
done it

☐ ☐ ☐ leave a brown paper bag with "Dead dove. Do not eat" on it in your work fridge

☐ ☐ ☐ visit the village of Llanfairpwllgwyngyllgogerychwyrn- drobwllllantysiliogogogoch in Wales

☐ ☐ ☐ make mole sauce

☐ ☐ ☐ dip Persian *nan-e nokhodchi* chickpea cookies into chickpea milk

☐ ☐ ☐ go to SXSW for the gaming

☐ ☐ ☐ go to SXSW for the comedy

☐ ☐ ☐ go to SXSW for the films

☐ ☐ ☐ live in an A-frame house

☐ ☐ ☐ watch *The Shining* on Father's Day

☐ ☐ ☐ drive the Overseas Highway through the Florida Keys

☐ ☐ ☐ ban the use of the word "epic" in your presence

☐ ☐ ☐ eat at Potato Head in Katamama, Bali

bucket	f*ck it	done it

☐ ☐ ☐ create a scratch and sniff sticker that smells like your partner

☐ ☐ ☐ eat Korean fried chicken instead of the Kentucky version

☐ ☐ ☐ try skysurfing

☐ ☐ ☐ fall into a freshly raked pile of leaves

☐ ☐ ☐ save ten per cent of every pay cheque

☐ ☐ ☐ dive down the Molinere Underwater Sculpture Park in Grenada

☐ ☐ ☐ visit Harlem in New York

☐ ☐ ☐ visit Haarlem in the Netherlands

☐ ☐ ☐ compete in memory sports

☐ ☐ ☐ enter the World Memory Championships

☐ ☐ ☐ experiment with teledildonics

☐ ☐ ☐ practise yin yoga

☐ ☐ ☐ hear Silbo Gomero, the whistling language used in the Canary Islands

☐ ☐ ☐ install surround sound in your TV room

☐ ☐ ☐ save an old horse headed to the glue factory

☐ ☐ ☐ enter the Barkley Marathons

☐ ☐ ☐ go to a *kräftskiva*, a crayfish party in Sweden

☐ ☐ ☐ go to a crawfish boil in Louisiana

☐ ☐ ☐ buy a Navajo rug

☐ ☐ ☐ rent your extra room on Airbnb

☐ ☐ ☐ bring someone breakfast in bed

☐ ☐ ☐ use an air horn to get your kids' attention

☐ ☐ ☐ see the fairy chimneys in Cappadocia, Turkey

☐ ☐ ☐ drink a rum punch at Basil's Bar on Mustique

☐ ☐ ☐ throw a sausage party to celebrate UK Sausage Week

☐ ☐ ☐ stroll through a park with a parasol in hand

☐ ☐ ☐ visit Tokyo and subsist solely on vending machine fare

☐ ☐ ☐ carry a clutch clutch

☐ ☐ ☐ don't pretend that your middlebrow predilections are anything but

☐ ☐ ☐ eat a fluffernutter sandwich

☐ ☐ ☐ hold an MTV Movie Award in your hand

☐ ☐ ☐ admit you're a Royal Watcher

☐ ☐ ☐ listen to Wu-Tang Clan's *Once upon a Time in Shaolin* album

☐ ☐ ☐ write a Bildungsroman

☐ ☐ ☐ relive the 90s and tell someone to "talk to the hand"

☐ ☐ ☐ make boozy ice lollies

☐ ☐ ☐ wear Bermuda shorts in Bermuda

☐ ☐ ☐ get your fortune from a Zoltan fortune-telling machine

☐ ☐ ☐ go overlanding

☐ ☐ ☐ pet Lil Bub

☐ ☐ ☑ wear a mood ring

☐ ☐ ☐ eat head cheese

☐ ☐ ☐ meet Darwin – the Ikea monkey

☐ ☐ ☐ pick wildflowers

☐ ☐ ☐ form the perfect tie dimple

☐ ☐ ☐ tour the ruins of Pompeii, Italy

☐ ☐ ☐ see salmon spawning

☐ ☐ ☐ stay at the Crocodile Hotel in Jabiru, Australia

☐ ☐ ☐ kick impostor syndrome's ass

☐ ☐ ☐ dress like Faye Dunaway circa *Bonnie and Clyde*

☐ ☐ ☐ go tanking in Nebraska

☐ ☐ ☐ use a tool library instead of buying your own

☐ ☐ ☐ buy a courtroom sketch and put it on your wall

☐ ☐ ☐ join Kiva and give out microloans

☐ ☐ ☐ eat at a *vendéglo, étterem, étkezde, bisztró, büfé, lacikonyha,* and *kávéház* in Hungary

☐ ☐ ☐ buy a virtual reality headset

☐ ☐ ☐ try cryotherapy

☐ ☐ ☐ explore Noah Purifoy's Joshua Tree Outdoor Museum in California

☐ ☐ ☐ use the line "Did you just fart? Because you blew me away"

☐ ☐ ☐ get a foot massage from a prison inmate in Chiang Mai, Thailand

☐ ☐ ☐ prove Christopher Marlowe wrote Shakespeare's works and claim the Hoffman Prize

☐ ☐ ☐ ogle Paul McCarthy's *Santa Claus* statue in Rotterdam, Netherlands

☐ ☐ ☐ drink a glow-in-the-dark cocktail

☐ ☐ ☐ make gravy from scratch

☐ ☐ ☐ celebrate Star Wars Day

☐ ☐ ☐ watch a Hair Battle at the Bronner Bros. International Beauty Show in Atlanta, Georgia

☐ ☐ ☐ swap out maraschino cherries for Amarena ones

☐ ☐ ☐ stop at In-N-Out Burger before you fly out of LAX

☐ ☐ ☐ walk on a black sand beach

☐ ☐ ☐ backpack around India

☐ ☐ ☐ use a Ouija board

☐ ☐ ☐ ride the Canadian train from Vancouver to Toronto in Canada

☐ ☐ ☐ let your partner pick your outfits for a week

☐ ☐ ☐ see a naked mole rat in the wild

☐ ☐ ☐ make someone grin from ear to ear

☐ ☐ ☐ "follow a hippie to a second location" and see what happens

☐ ☐ ☐ refuse to work in a cube farm

☐ ☐ ☐ have your Twitter account verified

☐ ☐ ☐ get a snail facial

☐ ☐ ☐ climb Mauna Kea in Hawaii

☐ ☐ ☐ climb Mount Everest in the Himalayas

☐ ☐ ☐ flambé your heart out and make cherries jubilee for dessert

☐ ☐ ☐ call someone a "gadabout"

☐ ☐ ☐ walk across the thirty-five bridges that span the Seine in Paris, France

☐ ☐ ☐ adopt the Japanese practice of *hara hachi bu* at mealtimes

☐ ☐ ☐ start saying "let the wild rumpus start" before you have sex

☐ ☐ ☐ make a salad with thirty different ingredients

☐ ☐ ☐ go heli-fishing

☐ ☐ ☐ buy a Moroccan pouf

☐ ☐ ☐ snorkel the Scottish Snorkel Trail in Scotland

☐ ☐ ☐ people-watch from your front step

☐ ☐ ☐ drink Black Cow vodka made from milk

☐ ☐ ☐ be a baller

☐ ☐ ☐ spice a recipe with *panch phoron*

☐ ☐ ☐ eat a muffuletta in New Orleans, Louisiana

☐ ☐ ☐ sport an asymmetric hairdo

☐ ☐ ☐ watch a Jultagi performance in South Korea

☐ ☐ ☐ visit the Lego House in Billund, Denmark

☐ ☐ ☐ open a bag of crisps without your dog hearing

☐ ☐ ☐ see an animal bridge

☐ ☐ ☐ raft the Salmon River in Idaho

☐ ☐ ☐ dip your toes in the Balearic Sea

☐ ☐ ☐ learn the difference between cobblers, crisps, crumbles, betties, buckles, and pandowdies

☐ ☐ ☐ make one of each ⟍

☐ ☐ ☐ hack a meme

☐ ☐ ☐ drive by the *Brady Bunch* house in North Hollywood, California

☐ ☐ ☐ look at *shunga* instead of watching porn

☐ ☐ ☐ meet a Nobel Prize winner

☐ ☐ ☐ try sky flying

☐ ☐ ☐ watch the World's Ugliest Dog Contest in Petaluma, California

☐ ☐ ☐ sail the route Odysseus took in the *Odyssey*

☐ ☐ ☐ eat sea urchin

☐ ☐ ☐ land a McTwist on your snowboard

☐ ☐ ☐ attend a Gullah festival in South Carolina

☐ ☐ ☐ slay at your school reunion

☐ ☐ ☐ ride a horse topless à la Lady Godiva

☐ ☐ ☐ listen to country rap

☐ ☐ ☐ learn to speak Afrikaans

☐ ☐ ☐ see Gaudí's Sagrada Família in
Barcelona, Spain

☐ ☐ ☐ enter the 24 Hours of Horseshoe Hell climbing
competition in Arkansas

☐ ☐ ☐ buy a full set of Le Creuset cookware

☐ ☐ ☐ collect playing cards from different casinos

☐ ☐ ☐ visit the original Woodstock site in Bethel,
New York

☐ ☐ ☐ refer to dates as "nature's candy"

☐ ☐ ☐ realise the ego serves no purpose but its own

☐ ☐ ☐ bite into some grilled piranha

☐ ☐ ☐ watch the Tour de France live

☐ ☐ ☐ bike one leg of the Tour de France on your
own for fun

☐ ☐ ☐ attend the German Film Awards in
Berlin, Germany

☐ ☐ ☐ attend the National Film Awards in
New Delhi, India

☐ ☐ ☐ attend the Ariel Awards in
Mexico City, Mexico

☐ ☐ ☐ build a giant Jenga set for your back garden

☐ ☐ ☐ meal plan like a grown-up

☐ ☐ ☐ drink cold brew coffee all year long

☐ ☐ ☐ plant a tree over your placenta after
giving birth

☐ ☐ ☐ eat your placenta after giving birth

☐ ☐ ☐ experience weightlessness in a vomit comet

☐ ☐ ☐ cruise the Rhine

☐ ☐ ☐ do the Stanky Legg

☐ ☐ ☐ wear a velour suit (never of the track variety)

☐ ☐ ☐ date a goth

☐ ☐ ☐ visit the Museum of Historical Chamber Pots
and Toilets in Prague, Czech Republic

☐ ☐ ☐ give a hearty "boo-urns" to voice
your displeasure

	bucket	f*ck it	done it

☐ ☐ ☐ ask a Finn if *kalsarikännit* really means "drinking at home alone in your underwear"

☐ ☐ ☐ make up an English word for "kalsarikännit"

☐ ☐ ☐ walk along Glass Beach in Fort Bragg, California

☐ ☐ ☐ kiss a stranger at midnight on New Year's Eve

☐ ☐ ☐ drive the length of the Cape to Cairo Road in Africa

☐ ☐ ☐ install a library ladder in your home

☐ ☐ ☐ see a sadhu in India

☐ ☐ ☐ drink *glou-glou* wine

☐ ☐ ☐ join a condom of the month club

☐ ☐ ☐ visit all of the islands in an archipelago

☐ ☐ ☐ perform burlesque

☐ ☐ ☐ watch a burlesque performance

☐ ☐ ☐ fish for zipper trout

☐ ☐ ☐ make your own almond milk

☐ ☐ ☐   listen to the blues in the Mississippi Delta

☐ ☐ ☐   stage an intervention for someone
                  wearing patchouli

☐ ☐ ☐   ride in a hot-air balloon

☐ ☐ ☐   watch all of Werner Herzog's movies

☐ ☐ ☐   eat Wiener schnitzel in Austria

☐ ☐ ☐   attend a Burns supper on Burns Night

☐ ☐ ☐   watch a rap battle

☐ ☐ ☐   enter a butter-carving competition

☐ ☐ ☐   have a Warhol-esque print of yourself made

☐ ☐ ☐   watch a fainting goat faint

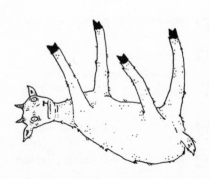

☐☐☐ visit Gerona, Spain, and pretend you're in Braavos

☐☐☐ go to Burning Man (but please don't refer to yourself as a burner)

☐☐☐ read the top one hundred greatest books of the twentieth century

☐☐☐ buy a Welsh lovespoon

☐☐☐ create your own list of your favourite one hundred books

☐☐☐ walk along Psycho Path in Traverse City, Michigan

☐☐☐ attend the Banff Mountain Film Festival in Canada

☐☐☐ get an *irezumi* tattoo

☐☐☐ get spanked when you summit Mount Triglav in Slovenia for the first time

DORCAS AVE

☐☐☐ go to a Louise Bourgeois exhibit

☐☐☐ find a street that shares your name

☐ ☐ ☐ drink a French 75 at Harry's New York Bar in Paris, France

☐ ☐ ☐ see the Chicago River dyed green for Saint Patrick's Day

☐ ☐ ☐ pee in your wetsuit

☐ ☐ ☐ admit that you're a brand whore

☐ ☐ ☐ dress up as Log Lady for Halloween

☐ ☐ ☐ watch the Emma Crawford Coffin Race in Manitou Springs, Colorado

☐ ☐ ☐ take part in *nantaimori* – eating sushi off a naked man

☐ ☐ ☐ take part in *nyotaimori* – eating sushi off a naked woman

☐ ☐ ☐ admire the sawdust carpets on Good Friday in Comayagua, Honduras

☐ ☐ ☐ see the Egyptian pyramids

☐ ☐ ☐ learn the difference between the bush and the outback

☐ ☐ ☐ make Gwyneth Paltrow's $200 smoothie

☐ ☐ ☐ eat chicken-fried steak

☐ ☐ ☐ meet a throuple

☐ ☐ ☐ stand inside a dung hut

☐ ☐ ☐ taste turtle soup

☐ ☐ ☐ skeet shoot

☐ ☐ ☐ replace your regular light bulbs with
Edison ones

☐ ☐ ☐ visit Dollywood in Pigeon's Forge, Tennessee

☐ ☐ ☐ stay at the GoldenEye Resort in Oracabessa, Jamaica

☐ ☐ ☐ smoke a joint with Seth Rogen

☐ ☐ ☐ visit the former leper colony on Spinalonga in Greece

☐ ☐ ☐ get wet on the natural waterslides at Slide Rock State Park in Arizona

☐ ☐ ☐ get your book published

☐ ☐ ☐ watch WrestleMania

☐ ☐ ☐ go to the Helsinki Baltic Herring Market in Finland

☐ ☐ ☐ eat a Nanaimo bar in Canada

☐ ☐ ☐ go to Costco and buy only one thing

☐ ☐ ☐ delete Candy Crush from your phone

☐ ☐ ☐ screen print your own T-shirt

☐ ☐ ☐ pay off your student loan

ECONOMY

MAYO

ENOUGH FOR THE WHOLE FAMILY!

bucket
f*ck it
done it

☐ ☐ ☐ drive across the sixteen-mile Jiaozhou Bay Bridge in China – the world's longest

☐ ☐ ☐ use the old "babe in the woods" routine to your advantage

☐ ☐ ☐ happy cry

☐ ☐ ☐ practise myomancy

☐ ☐ ☐ go berry picking

☐ ☐ ☐ give yourself a Korean foot peel

☐ ☐ ☐ see the Red Sarajevo Roses in Bosnia and Herzegovina

☐ ☐ ☐ launch a torpedo

☐ ☐ ☐ organise your books by colour

☐ ☐ ☐ sing a rowdy rendition of "I'm a Lumberjack and I'm OK"

☐ ☐ ☐ explore the Gion District of Kyoto, Japan

☐ ☐ ☐ play the tuba

☐ ☐ ☐ swear off fast food

bucket
f*ck it
done it

☐ ☐ ☐ futz

☐ ☐ ☐ have sex in a public place

☐ ☐ ☐ dine at Ithaa – the underwater restaurant –
in the Maldives

☐ ☐ ☐ swing from a vine à la Tarzan

☐ ☐ ☐ enter the World Cow Chip Throwing
Championship in Beaver, Oklahoma

☐ ☐ ☐ go somewhere in disguise

☐ ☐ ☐ see a puffin in the wild

☐ ☐ ☐ win at bingo

☐ ☐ ☐ watch cinema verité

☐ ☐ ☐ run the Gobi March

☐ ☐ ☐ usher in the dawn of camel toe acceptance

☐ ☐ ☐ use a sheet mask

☐ ☐ ☐ gather your cojones and eat *hakarl* in Iceland

☐ ☐ ☐ come up with a strong password on
the first try

☐ ☐ ☐ have your palm read

☐ ☐ ☐ meet a momager

☐ ☐ ☐ take a spin class

☐ ☐ ☐ teach your grandpa
to give the old finger guns

☐ ☐ ☐ hassle the Hoff and see what happens

☐ ☐ ☐ soak in the hot springs in Karlovy
Vary, Czech Republic

☐ ☐ ☐ eat cockles in Swansea, Wales

☐ ☐ ☐ become a spirulina devotee

☐ ☐ ☐ go to an art opening and pretend to be
the artist

☐ ☐ ☐ mull wine

☐ ☐ ☐ mull something over with wine

☐ ☐ ☐ join a sit-in

☐ ☐ ☐ try kiiking in Estonia

☐ ☐ ☐ collect penny dreadfuls

☐ ☐ ☐ choose your meal for death
row, even if you'll never be on it

☐ ☐ ☐ get into British kitchen sink realism

☐ ☐ ☐ make the Chef's Chocolate Salty Balls,
stick 'em in your mouth, and suck 'em

☐ ☐ ☐ stay up all night for Nuit Blanche in
Riga, Latvia

☐ ☐ ☐ set up a desktop computer instead of a
laptop at your local coffee shop and see
what happens

☐ ☐ ☐ visit Slickpoo, Idaho

☐ ☐ ☐ eat bourride and bouillabaisse in the
South of France and pick a favourite

☐ ☐ ☐ drink Ron Jeremy's Ron de Jeremy Rum

☐ ☐ ☐ island-hop in the Seychelles

☐ ☐ ☐ make a cauliflower pizza crust

☐ ☐ ☐ study pictish stones in Scotland

☐ ☐ ☐ read the very first issue of *Rolling Stone*
from 1967

bucket it
f*ck it
done it

☐ ☐ ☐ pet Grumpy Cat

☐ ☐ ☐ ask someone if their
"ass is jealous of all
the shit coming out
of their mouth"

☐ ☐ ☐ kiss your mother with that mouth

☐ ☐ ☐ tell someone they nailed it at the Tokyo Nail
Show in Japan

☐ ☐ ☐ organise a marshmallow-eating competition

☐ ☐ ☐ see a double rainbow

☐ ☐ ☐ climb the Matterhorn in Switzerland

☐ ☐ ☐ ride the Matterhorn at Disneyland in California

☐ ☐ ☐ pretend you have lachanophobia so you don't
have to eat your vegetables

☐ ☐ ☐ order the $1,000 Golden Opulence Sundae
at Serendipity 3 in New York, New York

☐ ☐ ☐ find proof that Sasquatches exist

☐ ☐ ☐ swim with a manta ray

□ □ □ adopt a meerkat as your emotional support animal

□ □ □ fake it until you make it

□ □ □ master an obscure dialect

□ □ □ flirt shamelessly with your waiter

□ □ □ try anti-gravity yoga

□ □ □ cry at a Beyoncé concert due to her overwhelming and undeniable perfection

□ □ □ wear a scarf bigger than Lenny Kravitz's

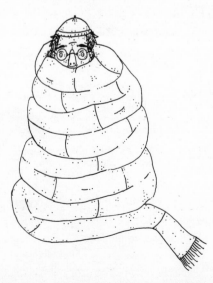

☐ ☐ ☐   stay in a cavern room at the Yanuk Evleri
Hotel in Cappadocia, Turkey

☐ ☐ ☐   ride the rotating tram up to San Jacinto Peak
in Palm Springs, California

☐ ☐ ☐   drink Muralski tea and see if it makes
you horny

☐ ☐ ☐   eat cornflakes and see if it makes you unhorny

☐ ☐ ☐   keep your hot takes to yourself

☐ ☐ ☐   see the Haenyeo divers in South Korea

☐ ☐ ☐   go to Las Vegas and order four club
sandwiches, four shrimp cocktails, one quart of
rum, and nine grapefruits from room service

☐ ☐ ☐   watch a guy fart himself to
death in the movie
La Grande Bouffe

☐ ☐ ☐   full ugly cry in public

282

bucket
f*ck it
done it

☐ ☐ ☐ describe something as Dickensian

☐ ☐ ☐ get a perm

☐ ☐ ☐ spend a week in Panama City, Florida

☐ ☐ ☐ spend three weeks in Queensland, Australia

☐ ☐ ☐ host a holiday cookie swap

☐ ☐ ☐ be the person your dog thinks you are

☐ ☐ ☐ dip your toes in the Celtic Sea

☐ ☐ ☐ eat Black Forest gateau in the Black Forest region of Germany

☐ ☐ ☐ attend the Peabody Awards

☐ ☐ ☐ meet an Amish person

☐ ☐ ☐ visit the Dr Pepper Museum in Waco, Texas

☐ ☐ ☐ try turkey bowling

☐ ☐ ☐ write a story that would scare Stephen King

☐ ☐ ☐ ask an interviewee, "How much wood would a woodchuck chuck?"

☐ ☐ ☐ make naan bread

bucket
f*ck it
done it

☐ ☐ ☐ have a threesome

☐ ☐ ☐ visit Cumbum, India

☐ ☐ ☐ practise Tonglen meditation

☐ ☐ ☐ go to a Basquiat exhibit

☐ ☐ ☐ see a therapist as an exercise in self-discovery, not an admission of failure

☐ ☐ ☐ convince someone that Elton John wrote a song about Tony Danza

☐ ☐ ☐ subject yourself to Shibari

☐ ☐ ☐ worship at the International Church of Cannabis in Denver, Colorado

☐ ☐ ☐ call carob what it is – the *Single White Female* of chocolate

☐ ☐ ☐ ogle the phallic houses in Bhutan

☐ ☐ ☐ reenact the Christopher Walken "Weapon of Choice" dance (minus the flying)

☐ ☐ ☐ attend the World Domination Summit in Portland, Oregon

☐ ☐ ☐ celebrate National High Five Day

☐ ☐ ☐ drink a cocktail out of a coconut

☐ ☐ ☐ carpe all of the diems

☐ ☐ ☐ git 'er done

b.y.o.b

(bring your own bucket)

bucket
f*ck it
done it

☐ ☐ ☐ _____

☐ ☐ ☐ _____

☐ ☐ ☐ _____

☐ ☐ ☐ _____

☐ ☐ ☐ _____

☐ ☐ ☐ _____

☐ ☐ ☐ _____

☐ ☐ ☐ _____

☐ ☐ ☐ _____

☐ ☐ ☐ _____

☐ ☐ ☐ _____

☐ ☐ ☐ _____

☐ ☐ ☐ _____

☐ ☐ ☐ _____

bucket
f*ck it
done it

☐ ☐ ☐ _____

☐ ☐ ☐ _____

☐ ☐ ☐ _____

☐ ☐ ☐ _____

☐ ☐ ☐ _____

☐ ☐ ☐ _____

☐ ☐ ☐ _____

☐ ☐ ☐ _____

☐ ☐ ☐ _____

☐ ☐ ☐ _____

☐ ☐ ☐ _____

☐ ☐ ☐ _____

☐ ☐ ☐ _____

☐ ☐ ☐ _____

☐ ☐ ☐ _____

bucket
f*ck it
done it

☐ ☐ ☐ _____

☐ ☐ ☐ _____

☐ ☐ ☐ _____

☐ ☐ ☐ _____

☐ ☐ ☐ _____

☐ ☐ ☐ _____

☐ ☐ ☐ _____

☐ ☐ ☐ _____

☐ ☐ ☐ _____

☐ ☐ ☐ _____

☐ ☐ ☐ _____

☐ ☐ ☐ _____

☐ ☐ ☐ _____

☐ ☐ ☐ _____

☐ ☐ ☐ _____

bucket	f*ck it	done it	
☐	☐	☐	_____
☐	☐	☐	_____
☐	☐	☐	_____
☐	☐	☐	_____
☐	☐	☐	_____
☐	☐	☐	_____
☐	☐	☐	_____
☐	☐	☐	_____
☐	☐	☐	_____
☐	☐	☐	_____
☐	☐	☐	_____
☐	☐	☐	_____
☐	☐	☐	_____
☐	☐	☐	_____
☐	☐	☐	_____

bucket	f*ck it	done it	
☐	☐	☐	_____
☐	☐	☐	_____
☐	☐	☐	_____
☐	☐	☐	_____
☐	☐	☐	_____
☐	☐	☐	_____
☐	☐	☐	_____
☐	☐	☐	_____
☐	☐	☐	_____
☐	☐	☐	_____
☐	☐	☐	_____
☐	☐	☐	_____
☐	☐	☐	_____
☐	☐	☐	_____
☐	☐	☐	_____

bucket	f*ck it	done it	
☐	☐	☐	_____
☐	☐	☐	_____
☐	☐	☐	_____
☐	☐	☐	_____
☐	☐	☐	_____
☐	☐	☐	_____
☐	☐	☐	_____
☐	☐	☐	_____
☐	☐	☐	_____
☐	☐	☐	_____
☐	☐	☐	_____
☐	☐	☐	_____
☐	☐	☐	_____
☐	☐	☐	_____
☐	☐	☐	_____

bucket
f*ck it
done it

☐ ☐ ☐ _____

☐ ☐ ☐ _____

☐ ☐ ☐ _____

☐ ☐ ☐ _____

☐ ☐ ☐ _____

☐ ☐ ☐ _____

☐ ☐ ☐ _____

☐ ☐ ☐ _____

☐ ☐ ☐ _____

☐ ☐ ☐ _____

☐ ☐ ☐ _____

☐ ☐ ☐ _____

☐ ☐ ☐ _____

☐ ☐ ☐ _____

☐ ☐ ☐ _____

bucket	f*ck it	done it	
☐	☐	☐	_____
☐	☐	☐	_____
☐	☐	☐	_____
☐	☐	☐	_____
☐	☐	☐	_____
☐	☐	☐	_____
☐	☐	☐	_____
☐	☐	☐	_____
☐	☐	☐	_____
☐	☐	☐	_____
☐	☐	☐	_____
☐	☐	☐	_____
☐	☐	☐	_____
☐	☐	☐	_____
☐	☐	☐	_____

bucket
f*ck it
done it

☐ ☐ ☐ _____

☐ ☐ ☐ _____

☐ ☐ ☐ _____

☐ ☐ ☐ _____

☐ ☐ ☐ _____

☐ ☐ ☐ _____

☐ ☐ ☐ _____

☐ ☐ ☐ _____

☐ ☐ ☐ _____

☐ ☐ ☐ _____

☐ ☐ ☐ _____

☐ ☐ ☐ _____

☐ ☐ ☐ _____

☐ ☐ ☐ _____

☐ ☐ ☐ _____

☐ ☐ ☐ _____

☐ ☐ ☐ _____

☐ ☐ ☐ _____

☐ ☐ ☐ _____

☐ ☐ ☐ _____

☐ ☐ ☐ _____

☐ ☐ ☐ _____

☐ ☐ ☐ _____

☐ ☐ ☐ _____

☐ ☐ ☐ _____

☐ ☐ ☐ _____

☐ ☐ ☐ _____

☐ ☐ ☐ _____

☐ ☐ ☐ _____

☐ ☐ ☐ _____

bucket	f*ck it	done it	
☐	☐	☐	_____
☐	☐	☐	_____
☐	☐	☐	_____
☐	☐	☐	_____
☐	☐	☐	_____
☐	☐	☐	_____
☐	☐	☐	_____
☐	☐	☐	_____
☐	☐	☐	_____
☐	☐	☐	_____
☐	☐	☐	_____
☐	☐	☐	_____
☐	☐	☐	_____
☐	☐	☐	_____
☐	☐	☐	_____

bucket
f*ck it
done it

☐ ☐ ☐ _____

☐ ☐ ☐ _____

☐ ☐ ☐ _____

☐ ☐ ☐ _____

☐ ☐ ☐ _____

☐ ☐ ☐ _____

☐ ☐ ☐ _____

☐ ☐ ☐ _____

☐ ☐ ☐ _____

☐ ☐ ☐ _____

☐ ☐ ☐ _____

☐ ☐ ☐ _____

☐ ☐ ☐ _____

☐ ☐ ☐ _____

☐ ☐ ☐ _____

bucket
f*ck it
done it

☐ ☐ ☐ _____

☐ ☐ ☐ _____

☐ ☐ ☐ _____

☐ ☐ ☐ _____

☐ ☐ ☐ _____

☐ ☐ ☐ _____

☐ ☐ ☐ _____

☐ ☐ ☐ _____

☐ ☐ ☐ _____

☐ ☐ ☐ _____

☐ ☐ ☐ _____

☐ ☐ ☐ _____

☐ ☐ ☐ _____

☐ ☐ ☐ _____

☐ ☐ ☐ _____

bucket
f*ck it
done it

☐ ☐ ☐ _____

☐ ☐ ☐ _____

☐ ☐ ☐ _____

☐ ☐ ☐ _____

☐ ☐ ☐ _____

☐ ☐ ☐ _____

☐ ☐ ☐ _____

☐ ☐ ☐ _____

☐ ☐ ☐ _____

☐ ☐ ☐ _____

☐ ☐ ☐ _____

☐ ☐ ☐ _____

☐ ☐ ☐ _____

☐ ☐ ☐ _____

☐ ☐ ☐ _____

bucket
f*ck it
done it

☐ ☐ ☐ _____

☐ ☐ ☐ _____

☐ ☐ ☐ _____

☐ ☐ ☐ _____

☐ ☐ ☐ _____

☐ ☐ ☐ _____

☐ ☐ ☐ _____

☐ ☐ ☐ _____

☐ ☐ ☐ _____

☐ ☐ ☐ _____

☐ ☐ ☐ _____

☐ ☐ ☐ _____

☐ ☐ ☐ _____

☐ ☐ ☐ _____

☐ ☐ ☐ _____

bucket
f*ck it
done it

☐☐☐ _____

☐☐☐ _____

☐☐☐ _____

☐☐☐ _____

☐☐☐ _____

☐☐☐ _____

☐☐☐ _____

☐☐☐ _____

☐☐☐ _____

☐☐☐ _____

☐☐☐ _____

☐☐☐ _____

☐☐☐ _____

☐☐☐ _____

☐☐☐ _____

☐ ☐ ☐ _____

☐ ☐ ☐ _____

☐ ☐ ☐ _____

☐ ☐ ☐ _____

☐ ☐ ☐ _____

☐ ☐ ☐ _____

☐ ☐ ☐ _____

☐ ☐ ☐ _____

☐ ☐ ☐ _____

☐ ☐ ☐ _____

☐ ☐ ☐ _____

☐ ☐ ☐ _____

☐ ☐ ☐ _____

☐ ☐ ☐ _____

☐ ☐ ☐ _____

bucket f*ck it done it

☐ ☐ ☐ _____

☐ ☐ ☐ _____

☐ ☐ ☐ _____

☐ ☐ ☐ _____

☐ ☐ ☐ _____

☐ ☐ ☐ _____

☐ ☐ ☐ _____

☐ ☐ ☐ _____

☐ ☐ ☐ _____

☐ ☐ ☐ _____

☐ ☐ ☐ _____

☐ ☐ ☐ _____

☐ ☐ ☐ _____

☐ ☐ ☐ _____

☐ ☐ ☐ _____

bucket
f*ck it
done it

□ □ □ _____

□ □ □ _____

□ □ □ _____

□ □ □ _____

□ □ □ _____

□ □ □ _____

□ □ □ _____

□ □ □ _____

□ □ □ _____

□ □ □ _____

□ □ □ _____

□ □ □ _____

□ □ □ _____

□ □ □ _____

□ □ □ _____

bucket
f*ck it
done it

☐ ☐ ☐ _____

☐ ☐ ☐ _____

☐ ☐ ☐ _____

☐ ☐ ☐ _____

☐ ☐ ☐ _____

☐ ☐ ☐ _____

☐ ☐ ☐ _____

☐ ☐ ☐ _____

☐ ☐ ☐ _____

☐ ☐ ☐ _____

☐ ☐ ☐ _____

☐ ☐ ☐ _____

☐ ☐ ☐ _____

☐ ☐ ☐ _____

☐ ☐ ☐ _____

bucket
f*ck it
done it

☐ ☐ ☐ _____

☐ ☐ ☐ _____

☐ ☐ ☐ _____

☐ ☐ ☐ _____

☐ ☐ ☐ _____

☐ ☐ ☐ _____

☐ ☐ ☐ _____

☐ ☐ ☐ _____

☐ ☐ ☐ _____

☐ ☐ ☐ _____

☐ ☐ ☐ _____

☐ ☐ ☐ _____

☐ ☐ ☐ _____

☐ ☐ ☐ _____

☐ ☐ ☐ _____

bucket
f*ck it
done it

☐ ☐ ☐ _____

☐ ☐ ☐ _____

☐ ☐ ☐ _____

☐ ☐ ☐ _____

☐ ☐ ☐ _____

☐ ☐ ☐ _____

☐ ☐ ☐ _____

☐ ☐ ☐ _____

☐ ☐ ☐ _____

☐ ☐ ☐ _____

☐ ☐ ☐ _____

☐ ☐ ☐ _____

☐ ☐ ☐ _____

☐ ☐ ☐ _____

bucket

f*ck it

done it

☐ ☐ ☐ _____

☐ ☐ ☐ _____

☐ ☐ ☐ _____

☐ ☐ ☐ _____

☐ ☐ ☐ _____

☐ ☐ ☐ _____

☐ ☐ ☐ _____

☐ ☐ ☐ _____

☐ ☐ ☐ _____

☐ ☐ ☐ _____

☐ ☐ ☐ _____

☐ ☐ ☐ _____

☐ ☐ ☐ _____

☐ ☐ ☐ _____

☐ ☐ ☐ _____

bucket
f*ck it
done it

☐ ☐ ☐ _____

☐ ☐ ☐ _____

☐ ☐ ☐ _____

☐ ☐ ☐ _____

☐ ☐ ☐ _____

☐ ☐ ☐ _____

☐ ☐ ☐ _____

☐ ☐ ☐ _____

☐ ☐ ☐ _____

☐ ☐ ☐ _____

☐ ☐ ☐ _____

☐ ☐ ☐ _____

☐ ☐ ☐ _____

☐ ☐ ☐ _____

☐ ☐ ☐ _____

bucket
f*ck it
done it

☐☐☐ _____

☐☐☐ _____

☐☐☐ _____

☐☐☐ _____

☐☐☐ _____

☐☐☐ _____

☐☐☐ _____

☐☐☐ _____

☐☐☐ _____

☐☐☐ _____

☐☐☐ _____

☐☐☐ _____

☐☐☐ _____

☐☐☐ _____

☐☐☐ _____

bucket
f*ck it
done it

☐ ☐ ☐ _____

☐ ☐ ☐ _____

☐ ☐ ☐ _____

☐ ☐ ☐ _____

☐ ☐ ☐ _____

☐ ☐ ☐ _____

☐ ☐ ☐ _____

☐ ☐ ☐ _____

☐ ☐ ☐ _____

☐ ☐ ☐ _____

☐ ☐ ☐ _____

☐ ☐ ☐ _____

☐ ☐ ☐ _____

☐ ☐ ☐ _____

☐ ☐ ☐ _____

bucket
f*ck it
done it

☐☐☐ _____

☐☐☐ _____

☐☐☐ _____

☐☐☐ _____

☐☐☐ _____

☐☐☐ _____

☐☐☐ _____

☐☐☐ _____

☐☐☐ _____

☐☐☐ _____

☐☐☐ _____

☐☐☐ _____

☐☐☐ _____

☐☐☐ _____

☐☐☐ _____

bucket
f*ck it
done it

☐ ☐ ☐ _____

☐ ☐ ☐ _____

☐ ☐ ☐ _____

☐ ☐ ☐ _____

☐ ☐ ☐ _____

☐ ☐ ☐ _____

☐ ☐ ☐ _____

☐ ☐ ☐ _____

☐ ☐ ☐ _____

☐ ☐ ☐ _____

☐ ☐ ☐ _____

☐ ☐ ☐ _____

☐ ☐ ☐ _____

☐ ☐ ☐ _____

☐ ☐ ☐ _____

bucket	f*ck it	done it	
☐	☐	☐	_____
☐	☐	☐	_____
☐	☐	☐	_____
☐	☐	☐	_____
☐	☐	☐	_____
☐	☐	☐	_____
☐	☐	☐	_____
☐	☐	☐	_____
☐	☐	☐	_____
☐	☐	☐	_____
☐	☐	☐	_____
☐	☐	☐	_____
☐	☐	☐	_____
☐	☐	☐	_____
☐	☐	☐	_____